Guitar Chord Songbook

Michael Jackson

T0039931

Photo courtesy of Sony / ATV Music Publishing

ISBN 978-1-4950-0139-0

HAL•LEONARD®
CORPORATION

7777 W. BLUEMOUND RD. P.O. BOX 13819 MILWAUKEE, WI 53213

Visit Hal Leonard Online at
www.halleonard.com

Guitar Chord Songbook

Contents

Another Part of Me

Words and Music by
Michael Jackson

Melody:

We're tak-in' o - ver, _

Ebm7　Dbm7　Fm7b5　Bb7#5　Cb　E　Bb7

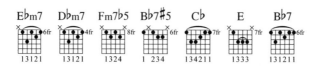

Intro　‖: Ebm7 |　　| Dbm7 | Fm7b5　Bb7#5 :‖

Verse 1

　　　　　　　Ebm7
We're takin' o - ver, we have the truth.

　　　　　　　Dbm7　　　　　　　**Fm7b5**
This is the mission, to see it through.

Bb7#5　　　　　**Ebm7**
　Don't point your finger, not dangerous.

　　　　　　Dbm7　　　　　　　**Fm7b5　Bb7#5**
This is our planet, you're one of us.

Chorus 1

　　　　　　　　　Cb　　　**Ebm7**
We're send - in' out a ma - jor love,

　　　　　　Cb　　　　　　　　　**Ebm7**
And this ____ is our message to you. ____ (Message to you.)

　　　　　　　　　　E　　　　　　　**Ebm7**
The planets are lin - in' up, we're bringin' bright - er days.

　　　　　Fm7b5　　　　　　　　**Bb7**
They're all ____ in line waitin' for you, ____ can't you see?

Bb7#5　N.C.　　　　　　　　　**Ebm7**　　　　　**Dbm7**
　　　You're just another part of me, hee, hee! Ooh.

Verse 2

Fm7b5 Bb7#5   Ebm7
          Out from a na - tion, I feel the truth.

    Dbm7   Fm7b5
The final message we'll bring to you.

Bb7#5   Ebm7
  There is no danger to feel the truth.

       Dbm7   Fm7b5 Bb7#5
So, come a - gain, we need you.

Chorus 2

       Cb   Ebm7
We're send - in' out a ma - jor love,

   Cb   Ebm7
And this ____ is our message to you. ____ (Message to you.)

       E   Ebm7
The planets are lin - in' up, we're bringin' bright - er days.

   Fm7b5   Bb7
They're all ____ in line waitin' for you, ____ sho' 'nuff true.

Bb7#5 N.C.   Ebm7   Dbm7
    You're just another part of me, hee, hee! Ooh.

Fm7b5 Bb7#5
    Do, do, do, do, do.

Interlude

| Ebm7 | | | Dbm7 | Fm7b5 Bb7#5 | |
| Ebm7 | | | | | |

Instrumental   *Repeat Verse 1 (Instrumental)*

Chorus 3   *Repeat Chorus 1*

Outro

   Fm7b5 Bb7#5   Ebm7 Dbm7
‖:   An - other part of me.   :‖ ***Repeat and fade***
                                    w/ vocal ad lib.

Bad

Words and Music by
Michael Jackson

(Capo 1st fret)

Am7   D   Bm7   C#m7   E7#9

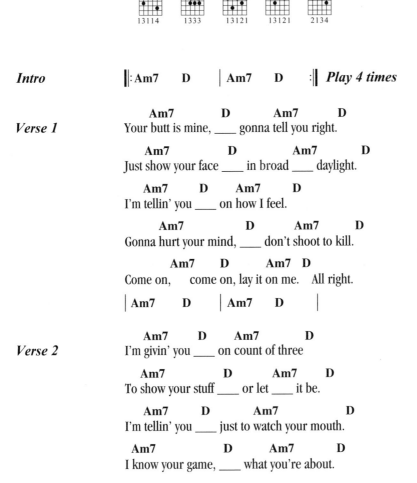

Intro

‖: Am7   D | Am7   D   :‖ *Play 4 times*

Verse 1

     Am7   D   Am7   D
Your butt is mine, ____ gonna tell you right.

     Am7   D   Am7   D
Just show your face ____ in broad ____ daylight.

     Am7   D   Am7   D
I'm tellin' you ____ on how I feel.

      Am7   D   Am7   D
Gonna hurt your mind, ____ don't shoot to kill.

      Am7   D   Am7 D
Come on,   come on, lay it on me.   All right.

| Am7   D | Am7   D |

Verse 2

    Am7   D   Am7   D
I'm givin' you ____ on count of three

    Am7   D   Am7   D
To show your stuff ____ or let ____ it be.

    Am7   D   Am7   D
I'm tellin' you ____ just to watch your mouth.

 Am7   D   Am7   D
I know your game, ____ what you're about.

Pre-Chorus 1

    Bm7   **C#m7**
Well, they say the sky's the limit,

   Bm7   **C#m7**
And to me that's really true.

   Bm7   **C#m7**
But my friend you have seen ___ nothin',

   E7#9
Just wait 'til I get through.

Chorus 1

     Am7 **D** **Am7**   **D**
Because I'm bad, I'm bad. (Really, really bad.)

       Am7 **D** **Am7**   **D**
You know I'm bad, I'm bad. (Really, really bad.)

       Am7 **D** **Am7**   **D**
You know I'm bad, I'm bad. (Really, really bad.)

    Am7   **D**
And the whole world has to an - swer right now

    Am7   **D** **N.C.**
Just to tell you once again. ___ *Who's bad?*

Interlude 1

‖: Am7 D | Am7 D :‖

Verse 3

    Am7   **D**   **Am7**   **D**
The word is out, ___ you're doin' wrong.

    Am7   **D**   **Am7**   **D**
Gonna lock you up ___ before ___ too long.

    Am7   **D**   **Am7**   **D**
Your lyin' eyes ___ gonna tell you right.

    Am7   **D**   **Am7**   **D**
So, listen up, ___ don't make a fight.

    Am7   **D**   **Am7**   **D**
Your talk is cheap, ___ you're not a man.

     Am7   **D**   **Am7**   **D**
You're throwin' stones ___ to hide ___ your hands.

Pre-Chorus 2   *Repeat Pre-Chorus 1*

Chorus 2   *Repeat Chorus 1*

Interlude 2   *Repeat Interlude 1*

Organ Solo   ‖: Am7   D | Am7   D   :‖ *Play 4 times*

Pre-Chorus 3

        Bm7   **C#m7**
We could change the world to - morrow,

        Bm7   **C#m7**
This could be a better place.

     Bm7   **C#m7**
If you don't like what I'm sayin',

     E7#9
Then won't you slap my face?

Chorus 3

            Am7   **D**   **Am7**   **D**
Because I'm ‖: bad, I'm bad. (Really, really bad.)

            Am7   **D**   **Am7**   **D**
You know I'm bad, I'm bad. (Really, really bad.)

            Am7   **D**   **Am7**   **D**
You know I'm bad, I'm bad. (Really, really bad.)

        Am7   **D**
And the whole world has to an - swer right now

        Am7   **D**
Just to tell you once again. ___ You know I'm… :‖ *Play 3 times*

Am7   **D**   **Am7**   **D**
Bad, I'm bad. (Really, really bad.)

            Am7   **D**   **Am7**   **D**
You know I'm bad, I'm bad. (Really, really bad.)

            Am7   **D**   **Am7**   **D**
You know I'm bad, I'm bad. (Really, really bad.)

        Am7   **D**
And the whole world has to ans - wer right now

        Am7   **D** **N.C.**
Just to tell you once again. ___ *Who's bad?*

Black or White
(Rap Version)

Words and Music by Michael Jackson
Rap Lyrics by Bill Bottrell

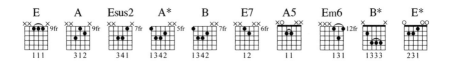

I took my ba - by on a Sat - ur - day date.

E   A   Esus2   A*   B   E7   A5   Em6   B*   E*

Intro
```
||: N.C.(E)  A  E |Esus2  E |N.C.(E)   A  E |Esus2  E :||
```

Verse 1
```
    N.C.(E)  A           E      Esus2   E
         I took my ba - by on a Saturday date.

    N.C.(E)  A           E
         But is that girl with you?

            Esus2      E
    Yes, we're one and the same.

        A*  N.C.
    Now I     believe in miracles

        A*    N.C.                    N.C.(E)  A
    And a mira - cle has happened tonight.

    E        Esus2
    Hee, ah,     ah.

    E          B      N.C.
    But if you're think - in' about my baby,

            A*   N.C.
    It don't mat - ter if you're black or white.
```

Interlude 1
```
|N.C.(E)  A  E |Esus2  E |N.C.(E)   A  E |Esus2  E  |
```

Verse 2	E A E Esus2 E A E

Verse 2

E A   E   Esus2 E A E
They print my mes - sage in the Saturday Sun.
  A   E   Esus2   E
I had to tell 'em I ain't second to none.
     A* N.C.
And I told about equality.
     A* N.C.   E A
And it's true, either you're wrong or you're right.
E   Esus2 E   B   N.C.
Oo, da,   ah, but if you're think - ing about my baby,
     A* N.C.
It don't mat - ter if you're black or white.

Interlude 2

|E A E |Esus2 E A E| A E |Esus2 E A E|
| A E |Esus2 E A E| A E |Esus2 E |

Bridge

E
I am tired of this yellin', I am tired of this stuff.

I am tired of this bus'ness. Go when the goin' gets rough.
 E7   A5
I ain't scared of your brother. I ain't scared of no sheets.
E7   A5 N.C.
I ain't scared of nobody. Don't put your finger in me.
               Em6
Spoken Rap: Pro - tection for gangs, clubs and nations,

Causin' grief in human relations.

It's a turf war on a global scale.

I'd rather hear both sides of the tale.

See, it's not about races, just places, faces.

Where your blood comes from is where your space is.

I seen the bright get duller.
     N.C.
I'm not gonna spend my life bein' a color.

Verse 3

           A* N.C.
Don't tell me you agree with me

        A*   **E**
When I saw you kickin' dirt in my eye.

A   **E Esus2 E**   **B**   **N.C.**
  Hee, hee. ____ Da, but if you're think - in' about my baby,

      A* N.C.   **E A E Esus2**
It don't mat - ter if your black or white.

E   **B**   **N.C.**
I said if you're think - in' of bein' my baby,

      A* N.C.   **E A E Esus2**
It don't mat - ter if you're black or white.

E   **B**   **N.C.**
I said if you're think - in' of bein' my brother,

      A* N.C.
It don't mat - ter if you're black or white.

Outro

‖: **E**   **A E** |**Esus2 E A E** :‖ *Play 9 times w/ vocal ad lib.*
| **A E** |**N.C.**   **B* E*** |
| ‖

Beat It

Words and Music by
Michael Jackson

Melody:

They told him,"Don't you ev - er come a round here.

Tune down 1/2 step:
(low to high) Eb-Ab-Db-Gb-Bb-Eb

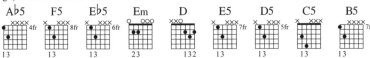

| Ab5 | F5 | Eb5 | Em | D | E5 | D5 | C5 | B5 |

Intro

N.C.(Ab5)			(F5)			
(Ab5)			(Eb5)			
N.C.						
			Em		D	
Em		D	Em		D	
Em		D				

Verse 1

E5   D5
They told him, "Don't you ev - er come around here.

E5   D5
Don't wanna see your face, you bet - ter disappear."

C5   D5
The fire's in their eyes, and their words are really clear,

E5   D5
So beat it. Just ____ beat it.

E5   D5
You better run; you bet - ter do what you can.

E5   D5
Don't wanna see no blood; don't be a macho man.

C5   D5   E5
You wanna be tough, bet - ter do what you can, so beat it.

D5
But you wanna be bad.

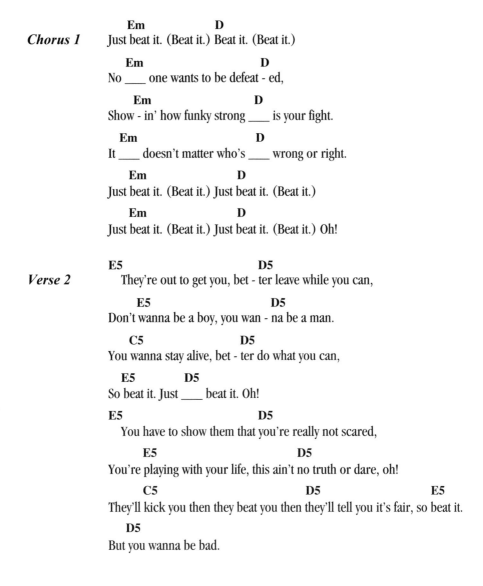

Chorus 1

      Em   D
Just beat it. (Beat it.) Beat it. (Beat it.)

       Em   D
No ___ one wants to be defeat - ed,

        Em   D
Show - in' how funky strong ___ is your fight.

        Em   D
It ___ doesn't matter who's ___ wrong or right.

       Em   D
Just beat it. (Beat it.) Just beat it. (Beat it.)

       Em   D
Just beat it. (Beat it.) Just beat it. (Beat it.) Oh!

Verse 2

E5   D5
   They're out to get you, bet - ter leave while you can,

     E5   D5
Don't wanna be a boy, you wan - na be a man.

     C5   D5
You wanna stay alive, bet - ter do what you can,

     E5   D5
So beat it. Just ___ beat it. Oh!

E5   D5
   You have to show them that you're really not scared,

     E5   D5
You're playing with your life, this ain't no truth or dare, oh!

      C5   D5   E5
They'll kick you then they beat you then they'll tell you it's fair, so beat it.

     D5
But you wanna be bad.

Chorus 2

     Em   **D**
Just beat it. (Beat it.) Beat it. (Beat it.)

     Em   **D**
No ____ one wants to be defeat - ed,

      Em   **D**
Show - in' how funky strong ____ is your fight.

     Em   **D**
It ____ doesn't matter who's ____ wrong or right.

     Em   **D**
Just beat it. (Beat it,) Beat it. (Beat it.)

     Em   **D**
No ____ one wants to be defeat - ed,

     Em   **D**
Show - in' how funky strong ____ is your fight.

   Em   **D**
It ____ doesn't matter who's ____ wrong or right. Just…

Bridge

E5				**D5**	
Beat it.		Beat it.			

E5				**D5**	
		Beat it.		Beat it.	

E5			**B5** **D5**	
			Beat it.	

E5				

Guitar Solo

```
‖: E5    D5 |      | E5    D5 |            |
 | C5    D5 |      | E5    D5 |         :‖
```

Outro-Chorus

      Em   **D**
‖: Beat it. (Beat it.) Beat it. (Beat it.)

      Em   **D**
No ____ one wants to be defeat - ed,

      Em   **D**
Show - in' how funky strong ____ is your fight.

      Em   **D**
It   doesn't matter who's ____ wrong or right.

      Em   **D**
Just beat it. (Beat it.) Beat it. (Beat it.)

      Em   **D**
No ____ one wants to be defeat - ed,

      Em   **D**
Show - in' how funky strong ____ is your fight.

      Em   **D**
It   doesn't matter who's ____ wrong or right.

Just… :‖ *Repeat and fade*

Billie Jean

Words and Music by
Michael Jackson

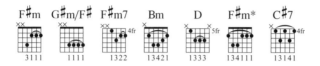

F#m	G#m/F#	F#m7	Bm	D	F#m*	C#7
××	××	×× 4fr	×	× 5fr	×	× 4fr
3111	1111	1322	13421	1333	134111	13141

Intro   ‖: N.C.(F#m) | | :‖

N.C.(F#m) (G#m/F#) (F#m7) (G#m/F#)
   Oo,   ooh,   ooh,   ooh.

(F#m) (G#m/F#) (F#m7) (G#m/F#)
   Oo,   ooh,   ooh,   ooh.

    F#m G#m/F#   F#m7 G#m/F#
Verse 1   She was more like a beau - ty queen from a movie scene.

    F#m G#m/F#   F#m7   G#m/F# Bm
    I said don't mind, but what do you mean I am the one

                        F#m G#m/F#
Who will dance on the floor in the round?

    F#m7   G#m/F# Bm
    She says I am the one

                      F#m G#m/F# F#m7 G#m/F#
Who will dance on the floor in the round.

    F#m   G#m/F#   F#m7   G#m/F#
    She told me her name was Billie ____ Jean, as she caused a scene.

    F#m   G#m/F#   F#m7   G#m/F# Bm
    Then ev - 'ry head turned with eyes that dreamed of being the one

                      F#m G#m/F# F#m7 G#m/F#
Who will dance on the floor in the round.

Pre-Chorus 1

D   F#m*
People always told me be careful what you do,

  D   F#m*
Don't go around breaking young girls' hearts.

  D   F#m*
And Mother always told me be careful who you love.

  D   C#7
Be careful what you do 'cause the lie becomes the truth. Hey!

Chorus 1

F#m G#m/F# F#m7 G#m/F#
Bil - lie Jean is not my lover.

F#m G#m/F# F#m7 G#m/F# Bm
She's just a girl who claims that I am the one,

        F#m G#m/F#
But the kid is not my son.

F#m7 G#m/F# Bm
She says I am the one,

        F#m G#m/F# F#m7 G#m/F#
But the kid is not my son.

	F#m G#m/F# F#m7 G#m/F#
Verse 2	For for - ty days and for - ty nights the law was on her side.

F#m   G#m/F#   F#m7   G#m/F#   Bm
But who can stand when she's in demand, her schemes and plans?

                                            F#m G#m/F#
'Cause we danced on the floor in the round.

F#m7   G#m/F#   Bm   F#m
So take my strong ad - vice: just remember to always think twice.

G#m/F#   F#m7   G#m/F#
(Don't think twice.) Do think twice.

F#m   G#m/F#   F#m7
She told my baby we danced 'til three

    G#m/F#   F#m   G#m/F#
As she looked at me,   then showed a photo.

    F#m7   G#m/F#   Bm
A ba - by crying, his eyes looked like mine.

                                    F#m G#m/F# F#m7 G#m/F#
'Cause we danced on the floor in the round.

	D F#m*
Pre-	
Chorus 2	People always told me be careful what you do,

        D   F#m*
Don't go around breaking young girls' hearts.

        D   F#m*
But she came and stood right by me, I took a smell of sweet perfume.

    D   C#7
This happened much too soon, she called me to her room. Hey!

Chorus 2

F#m G#m/F# F#m7 G#m/F#
Bil - lie Jean is not my lover.

F#m   G#m/F# F#m7   G#m/F#   Bm
She's just a girl who claims that I am the one,

                   F#m G#m/F# F#m7 G#m/F#
But the kid is not my son.

F#m G#m/F# F#m7 G#m/F#
Bil - lie Jean is not my lover.

F#m   G#m/F# F#m7   G#m/F#   Bm
She's just a girl who claims that I am the one,

                   F#m G#m/F#
But the kid is not my son.

F#m7   G#m/F#   Bm
She says I am the one,

                   F#m G#m/F# F#m7 G#m/F#
But the kid is not my son.

Interlude

‖: F#m   G#m/F# |F#m7   G#m/F# :‖ *Play 3 times*

F#m G#m/F# F#m7   G#m/F# Bm
              She says I am the one,

                   F#m G#m/F# F#m7 G#m/F#
But the kid is not my son.

Chorus 3

F#m G#m/F# F#m7 G#m/F#
Bil - lie Jean is not my lover.

F#m   G#m/F# F#m7   G#m/F#   Bm
She's just a girl who claims that I am the one,

                   F#m G#m/F#
But the kid is not my son.

F#m7   G#m/F#   Bm
She says I am the one,

                   F#m G#m/F#
But the kid is not my son.

F#m7   G#m/F#   F#m G#m/F#
She says I am the one,

F#m7   G#m/F#   F#m G#m/F#
She says he is my son.

F#m 7   G#m/F#
She says I am the one.

Outro

     F#m G#m/F# F#m7 G#m/F#
‖: Bil - lie Jean is not my lover. :‖ *Repeat and fade*

Dirty Diana

Words and Music by
Michael Jackson

Melody:

You'll nev-er make me stay, _ so take your

Gm   E♭   F

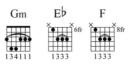

134111   1333   1333

Intro

| Gm | E♭ F | Gm | E♭ F |

Gm   E♭ F   Gm   E♭ F
Oh, no,   oh, no, ___ oh, no.

Verse 1

         Gm   E♭   F
You'll never make me stay, so take your weight off of me.
         Gm   E♭   F
I know your ev'ry move, so won't you just let me be.
         Gm   E♭   F
I've been here times before but I was too blind to see
         Gm   E♭   F
That you se - duce ev'ry man. This time you won't seduce me.
         Gm   E♭   F
She's saying that's okay. Hey, baby, do what you please.
         Gm   E♭   F
I have the stuff that you want. I am the thing that you need.
         Gm   E♭   F
She looked me deep in the eyes. She's touchin' me so to start.
         D   N.C.
She says there's no turnin' back. She trapped me in her heart.

Chorus 1

         Gm   E♭   Gm   E♭
Dirty Di - ana, no. ___ Dirty Di - ana, no.
         Gm   E♭   Gm
Dirty Di - ana, no. ___ Dirty Di - ana,
E♭   F
Let me be.

Interlude 1

Repeat Intro

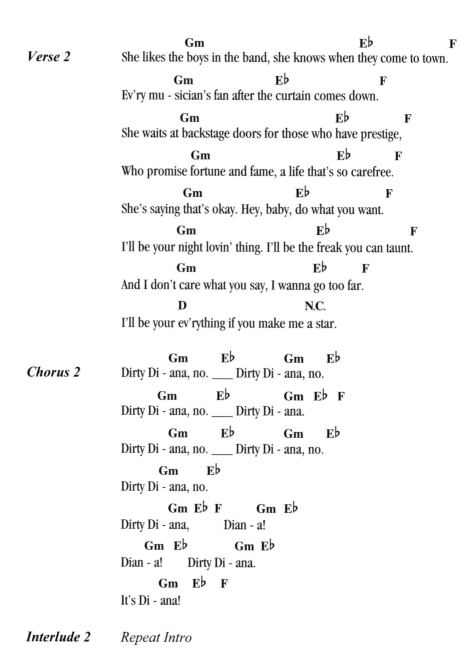

Verse 2

Gm   E♭   F
She likes the boys in the band, she knows when they come to town.

Gm   E♭   F
Ev'ry mu - sician's fan after the curtain comes down.

Gm   E♭   F
She waits at backstage doors for those who have prestige,

Gm   E♭   F
Who promise fortune and fame, a life that's so carefree.

Gm   E♭   F
She's saying that's okay. Hey, baby, do what you want.

Gm   E♭   F
I'll be your night lovin' thing. I'll be the freak you can taunt.

Gm   E♭   F
And I don't care what you say, I wanna go too far.

D   N.C.
I'll be your ev'rything if you make me a star.

Chorus 2

Gm   E♭   Gm   E♭
Dirty Di - ana, no. ___ Dirty Di - ana, no.

Gm   E♭   Gm   E♭ F
Dirty Di - ana, no. ___ Dirty Di - ana.

Gm   E♭   Gm   E♭
Dirty Di - ana, no. ___ Dirty Di - ana, no.

Gm   E♭
Dirty Di - ana, no.

Gm E♭ F   Gm E♭
Dirty Di - ana,   Dian - a!

Gm E♭   Gm E♭
Dian - a!   Dirty Di - ana.

Gm E♭   F
It's Di - ana!

Interlude 2   *Repeat Intro*

Verse 3

Gm   E♭   F
She said, "I have to go home, 'cause I'm real tired, you see.

Gm   E♭   F
But I hate sleeping alone. Why don't you come with me?"

Gm   E♭   F
I said, "My baby's at home, she's probably worried tonight.

Gm   E♭   F
I didn't call on the phone to say that I'm alright."

Gm   E♭   F
Diana walked up to me. She said, "I'm all yours tonight."

Gm   E♭   F
And then I ran to the phone saying, "Ba - by I'm alright."

Gm   E♭   F
I said,"But unlock the door 'cause I forgot the key."

D   N.C.
She said, "He's not comin' back, because he's sleepin' with me."

Chorus 3

Gm E♭   Gm E♭
Dirty Di - ana, no. ____ Dirty Di - ana, no.

Gm E♭   Gm E♭ F
Dirty Di - ana, no. ____ Dirty Di - ana, no.

Gm E♭   Gm E♭
Dirty Di - ana, no. ____ Dirty Di - ana, no.

Gm E♭   Gm E♭ F
Dirty Di - ana, no. ____ Dirty Di - ana.

Outro

Gm E♭   Gm E♭
‖: Come on! ____ Come on!

Gm E♭   Gm E♭ F
Come on! ____ Come on!   :‖ *Repeat and fade*

Don't Stop 'Til You Get Enough

Words and Music by
Michael Jackson

Love - ly _____ is the feel - in' __ now. __

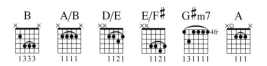

Intro

‖: B A/B | | B | :‖

Verse 1

B   A/B   B
Love - ly is the feelin' now.

    A/B   B
Fe - ver temp'ratures risin' now.

    A/B   B
Pow - er is the force, the vow

                A/B
That makes it hap - pen

            B
And there's no questions why.

            A/B   B
Ooh, get clos - er to my body now,

        A/B   B
Just love me 'til you   don't know how.

Chorus 1

            A/B
Ooh, keep on ____ with the force,

Don't, don't stop 'til you get enough.

       B
Keep on ____ with the force,

Don't, don't stop 'til you get enough.

       A/B
Keep on ____ with the force,

Don't, don't stop 'til you get enough.

       B
Keep on ____ with the force,

Don't, don't stop 'til you get enough.

Verse 2

B   **A/B**   **B**
Touch me and I feel on fire.

       A/B   **B**
Ain't noth - in' like a love desire.

       A/B   **B**
I'm melt - ing like hot candle wax.

     A/B   **B**
Sen - sation lovely where we're at.

       A/B   **B**
Ooh, so let love take us through the hours.

          A/B   **B**
I won't be complain - ing, 'cause this is   love power.

Chorus 2   *Repeat Chorus 1*

Interlude

```
||: B   D/E    E/F♯ |  G♯m7  A  B  :|| Play 3 times
|  B   D/E    E/F♯ |  G♯m7  N.C.    |
||: B   A/B          |                |
|  B                |              :||
```

Verse 3

B   A/B   B
Heart - break ene - my despise.

   A/B   B
Eter - nal love shines in my eyes.

     A/B   B
Ooh, so let love take us through the hours,

        A/B   B
I won't be complain - ing. Your love is   all mine.

Chorus 3

     A/B
||: Keep on ___ with the force,

Don't, don't stop 'til you get enough.

   B
Keep on ___ with the force,

Don't, don't stop 'til you get enough.

   A/B
Keep on ___ with the force,

Don't, don't stop 'til you get enough.

   B
Keep on ___ with the force,

Don't, don't stop 'til you get enough. :||

Verse 4

B   A/B B
Love - ly is the feelin' now.

      A/B
I won't be complain - ing,

   B
The force is   love power.

Outro-Chorus   ***Repeat Chorus 3 and fade***

The Girl Is Mine

Words and Music by
Michael Jackson

Amaj9 D/E F#7sus4 Bm7 Bm7/E Cmaj9 Fmaj E6 Bmaj9 E6/F#

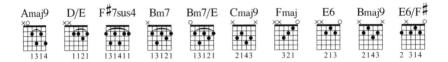

Intro   ‖: Amaj9 D/E | | Amaj9 D/E | :‖

Verse 1

     Amaj9   **D/E**
Ev'ry night she walks right in my dreams,

     Amaj9   **D/E**
Since I met her from the start.

     Amaj9   **D/E**
I'm so proud I am the only one

     Amaj9   **F#7sus4**
Who is special in her heart.

Chorus 1

        Bm7
The girl is mine,

Bm7/E   **Amaj9 D/E Amaj9 F#7sus4**
  The doggone girl is mine.

        Bm7
I know she's mine,

Bm7/E   **Amaj9 D/E Amaj9 D/E**
  Because the doggone girl is mine.

Verse 2

Amaj9   **D/E**
I don't understand the way you think,

Amaj9   **D/E**
Saying that she's yours, not mine.

Amaj9   **D/E**
Sending roses and your silly dreams,

Amaj9   **F♯7sus4**
Really just a waste of time,

Bm7

Chorus 2

Because she's mine,

Bm7/E   **Amaj9 D/E Amaj9 F♯7sus4**
 The doggone girl is mine.

     Bm7
Don't waste your time,

Bm7/E   **Amaj9 D/E Amaj9 D/E**
 Because the doggone girl is mine.

  Amaj9   **D/E**

Bridge

I love you more than he. (Take you an - ywhere.)

   Amaj9   **D/E**
Well, I love you endlessly. (Loving we ___ will share.)

   Cmaj9   **Fmaj7**
So come and go ___ with me, two on the town.

 D/E   **E6**
But we both cannot have ___ her,

 D/E **E6**
So it's one or the oth - er.

  D/E   **E6**
And one day you'll discov - er

  D/E
That she's my girl forever and ever.

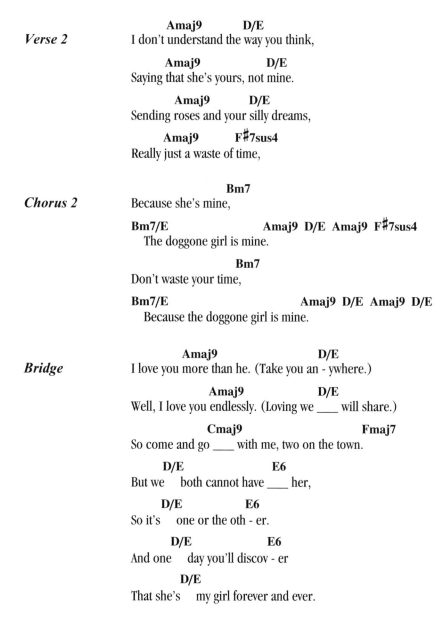

Verse 3

      Amaj9   D/E
Ah, don't build your hopes to be let down,

      Amaj9   D/E
'Cause I really feel it's time.

       Amaj9   D/E
I know she'll tell you I'm the one for her,

      Amaj9   F♯7sus4
'Cause she said I blow her mind.

Chorus 3

        Bm7
The girl is mine,

Bm7/E   Amaj9 D/E Amaj9 F♯7sus4
  The doggone girl is mine.

              Bm7
Don't waste your time,

Bm7/E   Amaj9
  Because the doggone girl is mine.

    D/E   Amaj9
She's mine. She's mine.

           D/E
No, no, no, she's mine.

      Amaj9   D/E
‖: The girl is mine. The girl is mine. :‖

      Amaj9   D/E
The girl is mine. (Mine, mine.)

      Amaj9   D/E
Yep, she's mine. (Mine, mine.)

      Amaj9   D/E
The girl is mine. (Mine, mine.)

      Amaj9   F♯7sus4
Yes, she's mine. Mine, mine.

N.C.   Bm7
Don't waste your time,

Bm7/E   Amaj9 D/E Amaj9 F♯7sus4
  Because the doggone girl is mine.

Outro

‖: Bmaj9 E6/F♯ | :‖ *Repeat and fade*
                                    w/ vocal ad lib.

In the Closet

Words and Music by
Michael Jackson and Teddy Riley

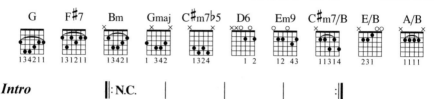

| G | F#7 | Bm | Gmaj | C#m7b5 | D6 | Em9 | C#m7/B | E/B | A/B |

Intro   ‖: N.C. | | | :‖

Verse 1
N.C.
She's just a lover who's doin' me by.

It's worth the giving, it's worth the try.

You cannot cleave it, or put it in the furnace.

You cannot wet it, you cannot burn it.

She wants to give it. (She wants to give it, ahh, she wants to give it.

She wants to give it, ahh, she wants to give it.

She wants to give it, ahh, she wants to give it.

She wants to give it, ahh, she wants to give it.)

Pre-Chorus 1
                    G   F#7   Bm
Whispered: One thing in life ___ you must understand,
Gmaj7   F#7   Bm
The truth of lust, woman to man.
Gmaj7   F#7   Bm
So, open the door ___ and you will see,
                    C#m7b5
There are no se - crets.
                                    F#7
Make your move, set me free.

Chorus 1

                      G   **F♯7**   **Bm**
Sung: Because there's something a - bout you, ba - by,

   D6   **Gmaj7** **F♯7**   **Bm**
That makes me want to ____ give it to you.

                G   **F♯7**   **Bm**
I swear there's something a - bout you, ba - by.

      Em9
Spoken: *Just promise me, whatever we say,*

      Gmaj7
Whatever we do to each other,

C♯m7♭5   **F♯7** **N.C.**
 For now, we make a vow to just   keep it in the closet.

Verse 2

             N.C.
If you can get it, it's worth a try.

I really want it, I can't deny.

It's just desire, I really love it.

'Cause if it's aching, you have to rub it.

She wants to give it. (She wants to give it, ahh. she wants to give it.

She wants to give it, ahh, she wants to give it.

She wants to give it, ahh, she wants to give it.

She wants to give it, ahh, she wants to give it.)

Pre-Chorus 2

           G   **F♯7**   **Bm**
Whispered: *Just open the door and you will see,*

Gmaj7   **F♯7**   **Bm**
 This passion burns inside of me.

Gmaj7   **F♯7**   **Bm**
 Don't say to me ____ you'd never tell.

           C♯m7♭5   **F♯7**
Touch me there, ____ make the move, cast the spell.

Chorus 2   *Repeat Chorus 1*

| *Interlude* | Bm | C#m7/B | Bm | E/B | |
| | Bm | A/B | Bm | A/B | |

                            G   F#7   Bm

Chorus 3   Because there's ‖: something a - bout you, ba - by,

         D6   Gmaj7 F#7   Bm
That makes me want to ___ give it to you.

                       G   F#7   Bm
I swear there's something a - bout you, ba - by,

         D6   Gmaj 7 F#7   Bm
That makes me want to ___ give it to you.   I swear there's :‖

G   F#7   Bm
Something a - bout you, ba - by,

      D6   Gmaj7 F#7   Bm
That makes me want to ___ give it to you.

                G   F#7   Bm
I swear there's something a - bout you, ba - by,

          Em9
That makes me want. *Spoken: Promise me, whatever we say,*

          Gmaj7
Whatever we do to each other,
C#m7♭5   F#7 N.C.
  For now, we make a vow to just   keep it in the closet.

         N.C.
Outro   She wants to give it.

        ‖: (She wants to give it, ahh, she wants to give it.) :‖ *Repeat and fade*

Heal the World

Words and Music by
Michael Jackson

There's a   place __   in your heart, __

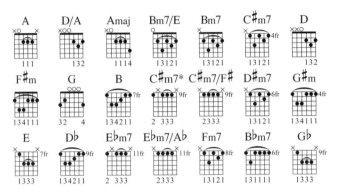

Intro | A D/A | Amaj7 D/A | A D/A | Amaj7 Bm7/E |

Verse 1

                 A   Bm7

There's a place ____ in your heart,

          C#m7   Bm7/E

And I know ____ that it is love.

                 A   Bm7   C#m7 Bm7/E

And this place ____ could be much bright - er than tomor - row.

             A   Bm7

And if you ____ really try

          C#m7   Bm7/E

You'll find there's ____ no need to cry.

               A   Bm7   C#m7 Bm7/E

In this place ____ you'll feel there's ____ no hurt or sor - row.

       Bm7   C#m7

There are ____ ways to get ____ there

     D   C#m7

If you care enough for the liv - ing.

     Bm7   Bm7/E

Make a little space, make a better place.

Chorus 1

                            A   **Bm7**
Heal the world, ___ make it a better place

    Bm7/E   **A**
For you and for me and the en - tire human race.

   C#m7   **F#m**   **C#m7**
There are   people dy - ing;

          D   **C#m7**
If you care enough for the liv - ing,

        Bm7   **Bm7/E**   **A D/A Amaj7 Bm7/E**
Make a better place for you and for me.

Verse 2

               A   **Bm7**   **C#m7**   **Bm7/E**
If you want __ to know why, ___ there's a love ___ that cannot lie.

              A   **Bm7**   **C#m7 Bm7/E**
Love is strong, ___ it only cares ___ with joyful giv - ing.

        A   **Bm7**
If we try, ___ we shall see

      C#m7   **Bm7/E**   **A**
In this bliss ___ we cannot feel ___ fear or dread.

      Bm7   **C#m7 Bm7/E**
We stop exist - ing and start liv - ing.

      Bm7   **C#m7 D**   **C#m7**
Then it ___ feels that al - ways love's enough for the grow - ing.

      Bm7   **Bm7/E**
So, make a better world, make a better world.

Chorus 2

                   A   Bm7
Heal the world, ___ make it a better place

  Bm7/E   A
For you and for me and the en - tire human race.

C♯m7 F♯m   C♯m7
There are   people dy - ing;

         D   C♯m7
If you care enough for the liv - ing,

     Bm7   Bm7/E   A
Make a better place for you and for me.

Bridge

          G   A
And the dream we were conceived in will reveal a joyful face.

          G   A
And the world we once believed in will shine a - gain in grace.

    F♯m   C♯m7
Then why do we keep strangling life,

          D   C♯m7
Wound this earth, crucify its soul?

       Bm7
Though it's plain to see, this world is heavenly.

Bm7/E
Be God's glow.

Verse 3

          A   Bm7   C♯m7   Bm7/E
We could fly ___ so high, ___ let our spir - its never die.

          A   Bm7   C♯m7 Bm7/E
In my heart ___ I feel you ___ are all my broth - ers.

           A   Bm7   C♯m7   Bm7/E
Create a world __ with no fear, __ together we'll __ cry happy tears.

           A   Bm7   C♯m7   Bm7/E
See the na - tions turn their swords into plow - shares.

     Bm7   C♯m7   D   C♯m7
We could ___ really get ___ there if you cared enough for the liv - ing.

     Bm7   Bm7/E
Make a little space to make a better place.

Chorus 3   *Repeat Chorus 2*

Chorus 4
      B   **C#m7***
Heal the world, ___ make it a bet - ter place

  C#m7/F#   **B**
For you and for me and the en - tire human race.

D#m7 **G#m** **D#m7**
 There are people dy - ing;

     E   **D#m7**
If you care enough for the liv - ing,

   C#m7*   **C#m7F#** **B**
Make a better place for you and for me.

Chorus 5
      Db   **Ebm7**
Heal the world, ___ make it a bet - ter place

  Ebm7/Ab   **Db**
For you and for me and the en - tire human race.

  Fm7 **Bbm7** **Fm7**
‖: There are people dy - ing;

   Gb   **Fm7**
If you care enough for the liv - ing,

   Ebm7   **Ebm7/Ab** **Db**
Make a better place for you and for me. :‖ *Play 3 times*

Outro
  Ebm7/Ab **Db** **Ebm7/Ab** **Db**
‖: You and for me, you and for me. :‖ *Repeat and fade*

Human Nature

Words and Music by
John Bettis and Steve Porcaro

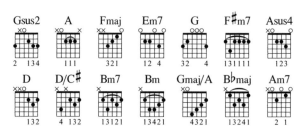

Intro

| Gsus2 A | | | Fmaj7 Em7 | | |
| Gsus2 | A | | Fmaj7 Em7 | | |

Verse 1

G   A G   A
Looking out   across the ____ night time,

G   A   G A
The city winks ____ a sleepless eye.

G   A G   A
Hear her voice   shake my win - dow;

G   F#m7 Em7 Asus4
Sweet seduc - ing sighs.

Verse 2

G   A G   A
Get me out   into the ____ night time.

G   A   G A
Four walls won't hold ____ me tonight.

G   A G   A
If this town   is just an ap - ple,

G   F#m7 Em7
Then let me take ____ a bite.

Chorus 1

A   G   A
If they say, "Why, why?"

D   D/C#   Bm7   A
Tell 'em that ____ it's hu - man na - ture.

G   F#m7   Em7
Why, why does he do me that way?

Bm7   G   A
If they say, "Why, why?"

D   D/C#   Bm7   A
Tell 'em that ____ it's hu - man na - ture.

G   F#m7   Em7   A
Why, why does he do me that way?

Verse 3

G   A G   A
Reaching out   to touch a ____ stranger,

G   A   G A
Electric eyes ____ are ev'rywhere.

G   A G   A
See that girl?   She knows I'm watch - ing.

G   F#m7 Em7
She likes the way ____ I stare.

Chorus 2

       A   G   A
       If they say, "Why, why?"

       D   D/C♯   Bm7   A
       Tell 'em that ____ it's hu - man na - ture.

       G   F♯m7   Em7
       Why, why does he do me that way?

       Bm7   G   A
       If they say, "Why, why?"

       D   D/C♯   Bm7   A
       Tell 'em that ____ it's hu - man na - ture.

       G   F♯m7   Em7
       Why, why does he do me that way?

Bridge

       Bm   Em7
       I like livin' this way.

       Bm   Em7   Bm Em7 Gmaj7/A
       I like lovin' this way.

Interlude

      |Gsus2 A| |Fmaj7 Em7| |
      |Gsus2 |A |Fmaj7 Em7| |

Verse 4

       G   A G   A
       Looking out   across the ____ morning,

       G   A   G A
       The city's heart ____ begins to beat.

       G   A G   A
       Reaching out,   I touch her shoul - der.

       G   F♯m7 Em7
       I'm dreaming of ____ the street.

Chorus 3

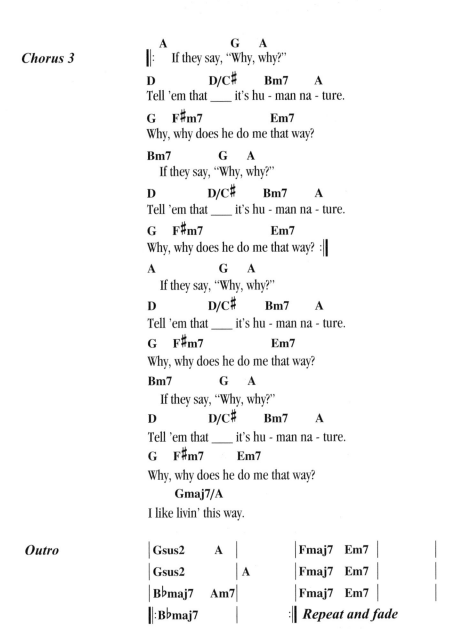

```
                A           G   A
||:    If they say, "Why, why?"

       D           D/C♯     Bm7      A
       Tell 'em that ____ it's hu - man na - ture.

       G    F♯m7              Em7
       Why, why does he do me that way?

       Bm7            G      A
          If they say, "Why, why?"

       D           D/C♯     Bm7      A
       Tell 'em that ____ it's hu - man na - ture.

       G    F♯m7              Em7
       Why, why does he do me that way?  :||

       A           G      A
          If they say, "Why, why?"

       D           D/C♯     Bm7      A
       Tell 'em that ____ it's hu - man na - ture.

       G    F♯m7              Em7
       Why, why does he do me that way?

       Bm7            G      A
          If they say, "Why, why?"

       D           D/C♯     Bm7      A
       Tell 'em that ____ it's hu - man na - ture.

       G    F♯m7        Em7
       Why, why does he do me that way?

                   Gmaj7/A
       I like livin' this way.
```

Outro

```
| Gsus2      A |        | Fmaj7   Em7 |              |
| Gsus2         | A     | Fmaj7   Em7 |              |
| B♭maj7    Am7|        | Fmaj7   Em7 |              |
||: B♭maj7      |       :|| Repeat and fade
```

I Just Can't Stop Loving You

Words and Music by
Michael Jackson

Melody:

Each time the wind _ blows,   I hear your voice, _

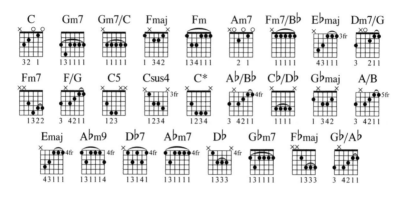

Intro |**C** | | | |

Verse 1

C
Each time the wind blows, I hear your voice,

Gm7
So   I call your name.

C
Whispers at morning, our love is dawning,

Gm7/C
   Heaven's glad you came.

Fmaj7
You know how I feel, this thing can't go wrong.

Fm   **Am7**
I'm so proud to say I love you.

Fm7/B♭
Your love's got me high, I long to get by.

E♭maj7   **Dm7/G**
This time is forever, love is the answer.

Verse 2

C
I hear your voice now, you are my choice now,

Gm7
The love you bring.

C
Heaven's in my heart, at your call I hear harps,

Gm7/C
And angels sing.

Fmaj7
You know how I feel, this thing can't go wrong.

Fm   Am7
I can't live my life without you.

Fm7/B♭
I just can't hold on. I feel we belong.

E♭maj7   Dm7/G
My life ain't worth living if I can't be with you.

Chorus 1

Gm7   C
I just can't stop loving you.

Gm7   C
I just can't stop loving you.

Gm7   Fm7
And if I stop, then tell me

E♭maj7   F/G
Just what will I do.

        N.C.   C5 Csus4 C*
'Cause I just can't stop loving you.

Verse 3

      C
At night when the stars shine, I pray in you I'll find

Gm7
  A love so true.

      C
When morning awakes me, will you come and take me?

Gm7/C
  I'll wait for you.

    Fmaj7   **Fm**
You know how I feel, I won't stop until I hear

                Am7
Your voice saying I do.

   Fm7/B♭
This thing can't go wrong. This feeling's so strong.

    E♭maj7   **Dm7/G**
Well, my life ain't worth living if I can't be with you.

Chorus 2

Gm7   **C**
  I just can't stop loving you.

Gm7   **C**
  I just can't stop loving you.

Gm7   **Fm7**
  And if I stop, then tell me

   E♭maj7   **F/G**
Just what will I do.

     N.C.   **C5**
'Cause I just can't stop loving you.

Bridge

Ab/Bb   Ebmaj7
We can change all the world tomorrow.

Cb/Db   Gbmaj7
We can sing songs of yesterday.

A/B   Emaj7
I can say, hey, farewell to sorrow.

Abm9   Db7
This is my life and I want to see you for always.

Outro-Chorus

Abm7   Db
‖: I just can't stop loving you.

Abm7   Db
I just can't stop loving you.

Abm7   Gbm7
And if I stop, then tell me

Fbmaj7   Gb/Ab
Just what will I do?   :‖   *Repeat and fade*

Love Never Felt So Good

Words and Music by
Michael Jackson and Paul Anka

Melody:

Ba-by, love nev-er felt so good. _

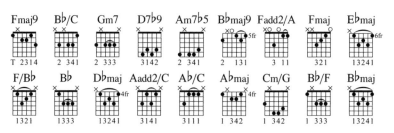

Fmaj9 Bb/C Gm7 D7b9 Am7b5 Bbmaj9 Fadd2/A Fmaj Ebmaj

F/Bb Bb Dbmaj Aadd2/C Ab/C Abmaj Cm/G Bb/F Bbmaj

Intro
‖: Fmaj9 | Bb/C | Fmaj9 | Bb/C :‖

Verse 1

Gm7 Bb/C   Fmaj9
Baby, love never felt so good.

  D7b9
And I'd doubt if it ever could,

  Gm7 Bb/C
Not like you hold me, hold me.

 Gm7 Bb/C   Fmaj9
Oh, baby, love never felt so fine.

  Am7b5   D7b9
And I'd doubt if it's ever mine,

  Gm7 Bb/C
Not like you hold me, hold me.

  Am7b5   D7b9
And the night ___ is gonna be just fine.

 Bbmaj9 Fadd2/A
Gotta fly, ___ gotta see,

  Gm7   Bb/C
Can't believe, ___ I can't take ___ it!

Chorus 1

      Gm7 **Bb/C**
'Cause, baby, ev - 'ry time I love you,

  Fmaj7   **D7b9**
In ___ and out my life, in ___ and out, baby.

Gm7   **Bb/C**
Tell me, if ___ you really love me

  Fmaj7   **D7b9**
In ___ and out my life, in ___ and out, baby.

   Gm7   **Bb/C**   **Fmaj9** **Gm7**
So, baby, yes, love never felt so good.

Verse 2

Gm7 Bb/C   **Fmaj9**
Baby, love never felt so fine.

    D7b9
And I'd doubt if it was ever mine.

      Gm7   **Bb/C**
Not like you hold me, hold me.

   Gm7 Bb/C   **Fmaj9**
Ooh, baby, love never felt so good.

   Am7b5   **D7b9**
And I'd doubt if it ever could,

    Gm7   **Bb/C**
Not like you hold me, hold me.

     Am7b5   **D7b9**
And the night, ___ gonna be just fine.

    Bbmaj9   **Fadd2/A**
Gotta fly, ___ gotta see,

      Gm7   **Bb/C**
Can't believe, ___ I can't take ___ it!

Chorus 2

Gm7   Bb/C
'Cause, baby, ev - 'ry time I love you,

Fmaj7   **D7b9**
It's in ___ and out my life, in ___ and out, baby.

Gm7   Bb/C
Tell me, if ___ you really love me

Fmaj7   **D7b9**
It's in ___ and out of love, driv - in' me crazy.

Gm7   Bb/C
Baby, yes, love never felt so good.

Interlude |Ebmaj7 |F/Bb Bb |Dbmaj7 |Abadd2/C Ab/C |
|Abmaj7   Cm/G D7b9 |Gm7 Bb/F |Ebmaj7 Bbmaj7 |Bb/C |

Verse 3

Gm7 Bb/C   **Fmaj9**
Baby, love never felt so fine.

        D7b9
And I'd doubt if it was mine, all mine.

        Gm7   Bb/C
Not like you hold me, hold me.

  Gm7 Bb/C   **Fmaj9**
Oh, baby, love never felt so good.

      Am7b5   **D7b9**
And I'd doubt if it ever could.

        Gm7   Bb/C
Not like you hold me, hold me.

        Am7b5   **D7b9**
And the night's ___ gonna be just fine.

      Bbmaj9   **Fadd2/A**
Gotta fly, ___ gotta see,

        Gm7   **Bb/C**
Can't believe, ___ I can't take ___ it!

Chorus 3

　　　　　　Gm7　Bb/C
'Cause, baby, ev - 'ry time I love you,

　　　Fmaj7　　　　　　　　**D7b9**
It's in ___ and out my life, in ___ and out, baby.

Gm7　　　**Bb/C**
Tell me, if ___ you really love me

　　　Fmaj7　　　　　　　　**D7b9**
It's in ___ and out of love, driv - in' me crazy.

　　　　Gm7 Bb/C　　　　　　**Fmaj9**
'Cause baby, love never felt so good.

　　Bb/C　　　　　　　　**Fmaj9**
Aw, ___ it's never felt so good.

　　　Bb/C　　　　　　　**Fmaj9**
So, no, ___ it never felt so good.

　　　　Bb/C　　　　　　　**Fmaj9**
Yeah, yeah, ___ it never felt so good.

　　　　Bb/C　　　　　　　**Fmaj9**
Uh, huh, ___ it never felt so good.

Man in the Mirror

Words and Music by Glen Ballard
and Siedah Garrett

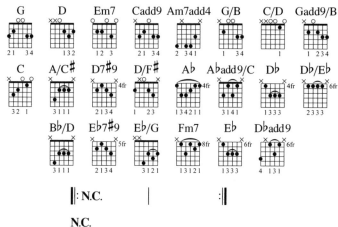

Intro   ‖: N.C.   :‖

Verse 1

N.C.
Gonna make a change, for once in my life.

It's gonna feel real good, gonna make a diff'rence,

Gonna make it right.

  G **D**
As I turn up the collar

 Em7 **D**   **Cadd9**
On ____ my fa - v'rite winter coat,

This wind is blowin' my mind.

     G **D**
I see the kids ____ in the street

 Em7   **D**
With not enough to eat.

  Cadd9
Who am I ____ to be blind?

Pretending not to see their needs.

Pre-Chorus 1

    Am7add4   **G/B**
    A summer's disregard,   a broken bottle top,

Cadd9   **G/B**
And a one man's soul.

    Am7add4   **G/B**
They follow each other on the wind, ya' know,

        Cadd9
'Cause they got ____ nowhere to go.

C/D
That's why I want you to know.

Chorus 1

G   **Gadd9/B**   **C**   **C/D**
I'm starting with the man in the mirror,

G   **Gadd9/B**   **C**   **C/D**
I'm asking him to change his ways.

G   **Gadd9/B**   **C**   **A/C♯**
And no message could have been any clearer.

    D7♯9
If you wanna make the world a better place,

                      G D/F♯ Em7
Take a look at yourself, and then make a change.

             D   **Cadd9**   **D Em7 D/F♯**
Na, na, na, na, na, na, na, na, na, nah.

Verse 2

G   **D/F♯**
I've been a victim of

Em7   **D**
A selfish kind of love.

Cadd9
It's time that I realize

     G   **D/F♯**
There are some with no home,

    Em7
Not a nickel to loan.

D   **Cadd9**
Could it be really me, pretending that they're not alone?

Pre-Chorus 2

  Am7add4   G/B
  A willow deeply scarred, somebody's broken heart,

 Cadd9   G/B
 And a washed out dream.

   Am7add4   G/B
 They follow the pattern of the wind, ya' see,

     Cadd9
 'Cause they got ____ no place to be.

 C/D
 That's why I'm starting with me.

Chorus 2

 G Gadd9/B C   C/D
 I'm starting with the man in the mirror,

 G Gadd9/B C   C/D
 I'm asking him to change his ways.

 G Gadd9/B   C A/C#
 And no message could have been any clearer.

   D7#9
 If you wanna make the world a better place,

 Take a look at yourself, then make a change.

Chorus 3

 G Gadd9/B C   C/D
 I'm starting with the man in the mirror,

 G Gadd9/B C   C/D
 I'm asking him to change his ways.

 G Gadd9/B   C A/C#
 And no message could have been any clearer.

   D7#9
 If you wanna make the world a better place,

            Ab
 Take a look at yourself, then make that change!

A♭add9/C   D♭   D♭/E♭
I'm starting with the man in the mirror,

A♭   A♭add9/C D♭   D♭/E♭
(Oh, yeah!) I'm asking him to change his ways.

A♭   A♭add9/C   D♭ B♭/D
(Better change!) No message could have been any clearer.

E♭7♯9
If you wanna make the world a better place,

Take a look at yourself and then make the change.

You gotta get it right, while you got the time.

                          A♭
When you close your heart, then you close your mind!

A♭add9/C D♭   D♭/E♭   A♭
With that man in the mirror, oh, yeah!

A♭add9/C D♭   D♭/E♭
I'm asking him to change his ways.

A♭   A♭add9/C   D♭ B♭/D
Better change! No message could have been any clearer.

E♭7♯9
If you wanna make the world a better place,

                      A♭
Take a look at yourself then make a change.

E♭/G Fm7   E♭   D♭add9
Hoo!   Hoo! ___ Na, na, na, na, na, na, na, na, na, nah.

A♭ E♭/G Fm7   E♭   D♭add9
Oh, yeah!   Na, na, na, na, na, na, na, na, na, nah.

Outro

D♭add9
‖: I'm gonna make a change. It's gonna feel real good! Come on!

(Change.) Just let yourself, you know. You've got to stop it.

Yourself! (Yeah! Make that change!)

I've got to make that change, today! Hoo! (Man in the mirror.)

You got to, you got to not let yourself, brother. Hoo! :‖ *Play 5 times*
                                          w/ vocal ad lib.

(Spoken:) Make that change.

Off the Wall

Words and Music by
Rod Temperton

Melody:

When the world is on your shoul-der, _____

Tune down 1/2 step:
(low to high) E♭-A♭-D♭-G♭-B♭-E♭

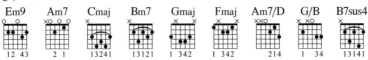

Em9	Am7	Cmaj	Bm7	Gmaj	Fmaj	Am7/D	G/B	B7sus4
12 43	2 1	13241	13121	1 342	1 342	214	1 34	13141

Intro |Em9 | | | |

Verse 1
             Em9
When the world is on your shoulder,

Gotta straighten up your act and boogie down.

If you can't hang with the feelin',

Then there ain't no room for you in this part of town.

'Cause we're the party people night and day,

Livin' crazy, that's the only way.

Chorus 1
          Am7   **Cmaj7**   **Bm7**
So, to - night, gotta leave that nine to five upon the shelf,
          Am7
And just en - joy yourself.
          Cmaj7   **Bm7**
Groove, let the madness in the music get to you.
          Am7 Gmaj7 Fmaj7
Life ain't so bad at   all.
Am7/D   **Em9**
  If you live it off the wall. ____ (Life ain't so bad at all.)

Live life off the wall. (Live your life off the wall.)

Live it off the wall.

GUITAR CHORD SONGBOOK

Verse 2

Em9
You can shout out all you want to,

'Cause there ain't no sin in folks all gettin' loud.

If you take the chance and do it,

Then there ain't no one who's gonna put you down.

'Cause we're the party people night and day,

Livin' crazy, that's the only way.

Chorus 2   *Repeat Chorus 1*

Bridge

Cmaj7   G/B
Do what you want to do,

        Am7   Am7/D
There ain't no rules, it's up to you.

        Cmaj7 G/B
It's time to come alive,

        Am7   B7sus4
And party on right through the night.

Verse 3

            Em9
Gotta hide your inhibitions,

Gotta let that fool loose deep inside your soul.

Want to see an exhibition?

Better do it now before you get too old.

'Cause we're the party people night and day,

Livin' crazy, that's the only way.

Chorus 3

      Am7   **Cmaj7**   **Bm7**
So, to - night, gotta leave that nine to five upon the shelf,

      Am7
And just en - joy yourself.

      Cmaj7   **Bm7**
Groove, let the madness in the music get to you.

      Am7 Gmaj7 Fmaj7
Life ain't so bad   at   all.

Am7/D   **Em9**
  If you live it off the wall. ___ (Life ain't so bad at all.)

Live it off the wall. (Live your life off the wall.)

Chorus 4

      Am7   **Cmaj7**   **Bm7**
So, to - night, gotta leave that nine to five upon the shelf,

      Am7
And just en - joy yourself.

      Cmaj7   **Bm7**
Groove, let the madness in the music get to you.

      Am7 Gmaj7 Fmaj7
Life ain't so bad   at   all.

Am7/D
  If you live it off the...

      Am7   **Cmaj7**   **Bm7**
To - night, gotta leave that nine to five upon the shelf,

      Am7
And just en - joy yourself.

      Cmaj7   **Bm7**
Groove, let the madness in the music get to you.   *Fade out*

P.Y.T.
(Pretty Young Thing)

Words and Music by
Quincy Jones and James Ingram

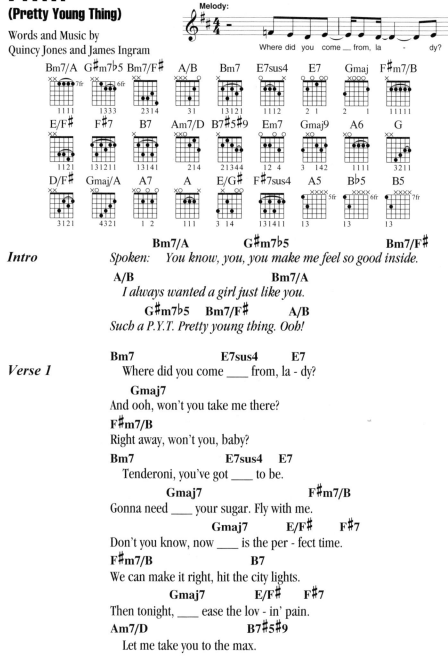

Intro

          Bm7/A   **G#m7b5**   **Bm7/F#**
Spoken: *You know, you, you make me feel so good inside.*

    A/B   **Bm7/A**
I always wanted a girl just like you.

    G#m7b5   **Bm7/F#**   **A/B**
Such a P.Y.T. Pretty young thing. Ooh!

Verse 1

    Bm7   **E7sus4**   **E7**
   Where did you come ___ from, la - dy?

     Gmaj7
And ooh, won't you take me there?

F#m7/B
Right away, won't you, baby?

Bm7   **E7sus4** **E7**
   Tenderoni, you've got ___ to be.

     Gmaj7   **F#m7/B**
Gonna need ___ your sugar. Fly with me.

          Gmaj7   **E/F#**   **F#7**
Don't you know, now ___ is the per - fect time.

F#m7/B   **B7**
We can make it right, hit the city lights.

       Gmaj7   **E/F#**   **F#7**
Then tonight, ___ ease the lov - in' pain.

Am7/D   **B7#5#9**
   Let me take you to the max.

MICHAEL JACKSON

Chorus 1

Em7   Gmaj9 N.C.
I wanna love you (P.Y.T.), pretty young thing.

A6   Em7 Gmaj9 N.C.
You need some lovin' (T.L.C), tender lovin' care,

A6   G D/F♯   F♯m7/B
And I'll ___ take you there,   girl.

B7   Em7   Gmaj9 N.C.
Ooh, I wanna love you (P.Y.T.), pretty young thing.

A6   Em7 Gmaj9 N.C.
You need some lovin' (T.L.C.), tender lovin' care,

A6   G D/F♯   F♯m7/B B7
And I'll ___ take you there.

  Gmaj7/A   A7
(An - ywhere you wanna go.)

Verse 2

Bm7   E7sus4   E7
Nothin' can stop ___ this burn - in'

  Gmaj7
De - sire to be with you.

F♯m7/B
Gotta get to you, baby.

Bm7   E7sus4 E7
Won't you come? It's emer - gency.

    Gmaj7   F♯m7/B
Cool my fi - re yearnin'. Honey, come set me free.

          Gmaj7   E/F♯   F♯7
Don't you know, now ___ is the per - fect time.

F♯m7/B   B7
We can dim the lights just to make it right.

     Gmaj7   E/F♯   F♯7
In the night, ___ hit the lov - in' spot.

Am7/D   B7♯5♯9
I'll give you all that I've got.

Chorus 2

           Em7   Gmaj9 N.C.
I wanna love you (P.Y.T.), pretty young thing.

A6   Em7 Gmaj9 N.C.
  You need some lovin' (T.L.C), tender lovin' care,

A6   G D/F♯   F♯m7/B   B7
  And I'll ____ take you there,   yes, I will.   Yes, I will.

           Em7   Gmaj9 N.C.
I wanna love you (P.Y.T.), pretty young thing.

A6   Em7 Gmaj9 N.C.
  You need some lovin' (T.L.C.), tender lovin' care,

A6   G D/F♯   F♯m7/B B7
  And I'll ____ take you there.

Interlude

‖: N.C. | | | :‖

Bridge

A   E/G♯ F♯7sus4
Pretty young things, repeat after me.

A5 B♭5 B5 N.C.   A5 B♭5
  Sing,   na, na, na. (Na, na, na.)

B5 N.C.   A5
Na, na, na, na. (Na, na, na, na.)

B♭5 B5 N.C.   A5
Sing,   na, na, na. (Na, na, na.)

B♭5 B5 N.C.   G
Na, na, na, na, na. (Na, na, na, na, na.)

D/F♯ F♯m7/B   B7
I'll take ____ you there, take you there.

Outro

Repeat Chorus 2 and fade w/ vocal ad lib.

Remember the Time

Words and Music by Michael Jackson,
Teddy Riley and Bernard Belle

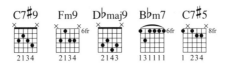

C7#9	Fm9	Dbmaj9	Bbm7	C7#5

Intro ‖: C7#9 │ │Fm9 │ :‖

Verse 1

    N.C.(C7#9)
Do you remem - ber when we fell in love?

    (Fm9)
We were   so young and innocent then.

    (C7#9)
Do you remem - ber how it all began?

    (Fm9)
It just   seemed like heaven, so why did it end?

Verse 2

    C7#9
Do you remem - ber back in the fall?

    Fm9
We'd be togeth - er all day long.

    C7#9
Do you remem - ber us holding hands?

    Fm9
In each oth - er's eyes we'd stare. Tell me.

Chorus 1

C7#9
Do you re - member the time when we fell in love?

Fm9
Do you re - member the time when we first met?

C7#9
Do you re - member the time when we fell in love?

Fm9
Do you re - member the time?

Verse 3

N.C.(C7#9)
Do you remem - ber how we used to talk?

(Fm9)
Ya know,   we'd stay on the phone at night 'til dawn.

(C7#9)
Do you remem - ber all the things we said?

(Fm9)
Like I   love you so, I'll never let you go.

Verse 4

C7#9
Do you remem - ber back in the spring?

Fm9
Ev'ry morn - ing the birds would sing.

C7#9
Do you remem - ber those special times?

Fm9
They'll just go on ___ and on in the back of my mind.

Chorus 2

Repeat Chorus 1

Bridge

Dbmaj9   Fm9
Those sweet ___ memo - ries

Dbmaj9   Fm9
Will al - ways be dear to me.

Dbmaj9   Fm9
And girl ___ no matter what was said,

Bbm7   C7#5
I will never forget what we had now, baby.

Outro-Chorus

C7#9
‖: Do you re - member the time when we fell in love?

Fm9
Do you re - member the time? :‖ *Repeat and fade*
w/ vocal ad lib.

Rock with You

Words and Music by
Rod Temperton

Melody:

Girl, ___ close ___ your eyes;

Tune down 1/2 step:
(low to high) Eb-Ab-Db-Gb-Bb-Eb

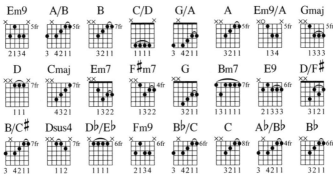

Intro

| Em9 | A/B B | Em9 | A/B C/D |
| Em9 | A/B B | G/A A | G/A A |

Verse 1

Em9   Em9/A   A/B
Girl, close ___ your eyes; let that rhythm get into you.

Em9   Em9/A   A/B
Don't try to fight ___ it, there ain't nothing that you can do.

Gmaj7   D
Relax your mind,

Cmaj7   G/A
Lay back and groove ___ with mine.

          Em7 F#m7 Gmaj7
You've gotta feel   that   heat,

N.C.
And a we can ride the boogie,

Em7 F#m7 Gmaj7 G A
Share that   beat   of love.

Chorus 1

           Em9   A/B B
I wanna rock with you, (All   night.)

Em9   A/B C/D
Dance you into day. (Sun - light.)

         Em9   A/B B
I wanna rock with you. (All   night.)

          G/A   A   G/A A
We're gonna rock the night away.

Verse 2

Em9   Em9/A   A/B
  Out on the floor there ain't nobody there but us.

Em9   Em9/A   A/B
  Girl, when you dance there's a magic that must be love.

Gmaj7   D
Just take it slow,

Cmaj7   G/A
 'Cause we've got so far ____ to go.

        Em7 F#m7 Gmaj7
When you feel   that   heat

And a we're gonna ride the boogie,
Em7 F#m7 Gmaj7 G A
Share that   heat   of love.

Chorus 2

         Em9   A/B B
I wanna rock with you, (All   night.)

Em9   A/B C/D
Dance you into day. (Sun - light.)

         Em9   A/B B
I wanna rock with you. (All   night.)

          G/A   A   G/A A
We're gonna rock the night away.

	Bm7 E9
Bridge	And when the groove is dead and gone

Bm7   E9
Bridge   And when the groove is dead and gone

                      Gmaj7   D/F♯
You know that love survives,

                Cmaj7   A
So we can rock forev - er.

Interlude |Em9 |A/B   B |Em9 |A/B C/D |
                     |Em9 |A/B B/C♯ Dsus4 |

                                 D♭/E♭
(I wanna rock with you, I wanna groove with you.)

         Fm9   B♭/C C
Outro-Chorus ‖: Rock with you, (All   night.)

Fm9   B♭/C D♭/E♭
Rock you into day. (Sun - light.)

         Fm9   B♭/C C
I wanna rock with you. (All   night.)

A♭/B♭ B♭   A♭/B♭ B♭
Rock the night away.   :‖ *Repeat and fade*
                                     w/ vocal ad lib.

Say Say Say

Words and Music by Michael Jackson
and Paul McCartney

Melody:

Say, say, _ say, ____ what you want

(Capo 1st fret)

Am7   D7   Dm7   F   E7#9   G

Intro

| Am7 | | D7 | Dm7 | | Am7 | |
| | | | D7 | Dm7 | | N.C.(Am7) |

Verse 1

Am7   **D7**
Say, say, say, what you want,

   Dm7   **Am7**
But don't play games with my af-fection.

           D7
Take, take, take what you need,

   Dm7   **Am7**
But don't leave me with no di-rection.

Chorus 1

   Dm7   **F**
All alone, I sit home by the phone

     Am7
Waiting for you, baby (baby).

Dm7   **F**
Through the years, how can you stand to hear

      E7#9
My pleading for you, dear?

         N.C.
You know I'm crying. Ooh, ooh, ooh, ooh.

| *Interlude 1* | |Am7 | D7 |Dm7 | N.C.(Am7) |

Verse 2

Am7   D7
Go, go, go, where you want,

  Dm7   Am7
But don't leave me here for-ever.

         D7
You, you, you, stay a-way,

  Dm7   Am7
So, long, girl, I see you never.

Chorus 2

  Dm7   F
What can I do, girl, to get through to you?

    Am7
'Cause I love you, baby (baby).

Dm7   F
Standing here baptized in all my tears.

    E7#9
Baby, through the years, you know I'm crying.

N.C.
Ooh, ooh, ooh, ooh, ooh.

Interlude 2 |Am7 | D7 |Dm7 | Am7 |

Chorus 3

     Am7 D7 Dm7
(You've got to say, say, say.)

        Am7
(You've got to say, say, say.)

Bridge

     G   **Am7**
You nev - er, ever worry,

G   **Am7**
And you never shed a tear.

        G   **Am7**
You're saying that my love ain't real

      E7$\sharp$9 **N.C.**   **E7$\sharp$9**
Just look at my face, these tears ain't drying.

Verse 3

Am7   **D7**
You, you, you, can never say

    Dm7   **Am7**
That I'm not the one who really loves you.

                      D7
I pray, pray, pray ev'ry-day

    Dm7   **Am7**
That you'll see things, girl, like I do.

Chorus 4   *Repeat Chorus 2*

Interlude 3   ‖:**Am7** | **D7** |**Dm7** | **Am7** :‖ *Play 4 times*

Outro

     Am7   **D7**
‖: (Ooh, ooh, ooh, say, say say.)

Dm7   **Am7**
(Ooh, ooh, ooh, say, say say.) :‖ *Repeat and fade*

Shake Your Body Down to the Ground

Words and Music by
Michael Jackson and
Randy Jackson

Melody:

I ____ don't know ___ what's gon - na hap - pen to ____ you, _

G7   F/G   G7/F

| | Intro | |: G7   F/G   G7/F | G7   F/G   G7/F :| *Play 4 times* |

Intro |: G7   F/G   G7/F | G7   F/G   G7/F :| *Play 4 times*

Verse 1

   G7   F/G G7/F
I ____ don't know what's gon - na happen

   G7 F/G G7/F
To ____ you, ____ ba - by,

   G7   F/G G7/F
But I do know ____ that

   G7   F/G G7/F
I love ____ ya.

  G7   F/G G7/F
You walk around this town

          G7   F/G G7/F
With your head all ____ up in the sky,

    G7 F/G G7/F
And I do know ____ that

    G7 F/G G7/F
I want ____ ya.

Chorus 1

      G7   F/G   G7/F
‖: Let's dance,   let's shout, *(Shout!)*

G7   F/G   G7/F
   Shake your bod - y down to the ground.

     G7   F/G   G7/F
Let's dance,   let's shout, *(Shout!)*

G7   F/G   G7/F
   Shake your bod - y down to the ground. :‖

Interlude 1

‖: G7   F/G   G7/F | G7   F/G   G7/F :‖

Verse 2

        G7   F/G   G7/F
You tease ___ me with your lov - in'

        G7   F/G   G7/F
To play hard ___ to ___ get

        G7   F/G G7/F
'Cause you do know ___ that

      G7   F/G G7/F
I want ___ ya.

    G7   F/G   G7/F
You walk around this town

             G7   F/G G7/F
With your head all ___ up in the   sky,

       G7   F/G G7/F
And you do know ___ that

      G7 F/G G7/F
I want ___ ya.

Chorus 2   *Repeat Chorus 1*

Interlude 2   ‖: G7   F/G   G7/F | G7   F/G   G7/F :‖ *Play 4 times*

Verse 3

        G7   F/G   G7/F
You're ___ the spark that lit ___ the fire

       G7   F/G   G7/F
Inside ___ of ___ me,

         G7   F/G G7/F
And you do know ___ that

        G7   F/G G7/F
I love ___ it.

     G7   F/G   G7/F
I need to do just some - thing

          G7   F/G G7/F
To get clos - er to your soul,

       G7   F/G G7/F
And ya do know ___ that

        G7   F/G G7/F
I want ___ ya.

Chorus 3   *Repeat Chorus 1*

Brass Solo   ‖: G7   F/G   G7/F | G7   F/G   G7/F :‖ *Play 4 times*

Verse 4

           G7   F/G   G7/F
You tease ___ me with your lov - in'

          G7   F/G   G7/F
To play hard ___ to ___ get

          G7   F/G G7/F
'Cause you do know ___ that

        G7   F/G G7/F
I want ___ ya.

     G7   F/G   G7/F
I need to do just some - thing

          G7   F/G G7/F
To get clos - er to your soul,

        G7   F/G G7/F
And ya do know ___ that

        G7   F/G G7/F
I want ___ ya.

Chorus 4

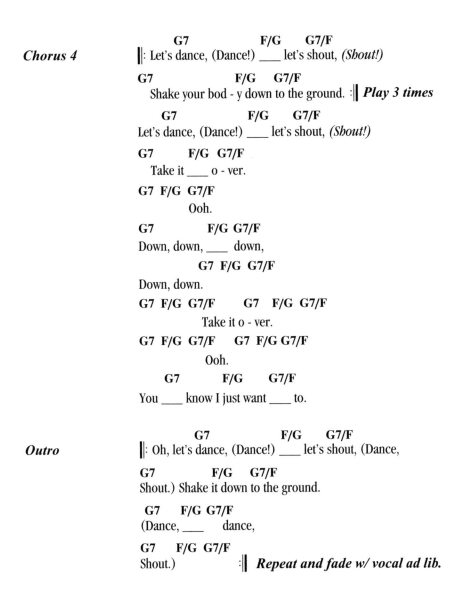

          G7   F/G   G7/F
‖: Let's dance, (Dance!) ___ let's shout, *(Shout!)*

G7   F/G   G7/F
  Shake your bod - y down to the ground. :‖ *Play 3 times*

    G7   F/G   G7/F
Let's dance, (Dance!) ___ let's shout, *(Shout!)*

G7   F/G G7/F
  Take it ___ o - ver.

G7 F/G G7/F
       Ooh.

G7   F/G G7/F
Down, down, ___ down,

          G7 F/G G7/F
Down, down.

G7 F/G G7/F   G7 F/G G7/F
          Take it o - ver.

G7 F/G G7/F   G7 F/G G7/F
         Ooh.

    G7   F/G   G7/F
You ___ know I just want ___ to.

Outro

           G7   F/G   G7/F
‖: Oh, let's dance, (Dance!) ___ let's shout, (Dance,

G7   F/G   G7/F
Shout.) Shake it down to the ground.

  G7   F/G G7/F
(Dance, ___ dance,

G7   F/G G7/F
Shout.)   :‖ *Repeat and fade w/ vocal ad lib.*

Smooth Criminal

Words and Music by
Michael Jackson

Melody:

As he came in - to the win - dow,

Am   G/B   C   G   F   E7sus4   E

Intro

| N.C.   Am | G/B | C   G   Am | G/B |
| C   G   Am | G/B | C   G   Am | G/B |
| C   G   Am |

Verse 1

   Am   G/B
   As he came into the window,

              C   G
It was the sound of a cre - scendo.

   Am   G/B
   He came into her a - partment,

              C   G
He left the bloodstains on the carpet.

   Am   G/B
   She ran underneath the table,

              C   G
He could see she was un - able.

   Am   G/B
   So she ran into the bedroom,

              C   G
She was struck down. It was her dorm.

Chorus 1

       F
"Annie, are you OK? So, Annie, are you OK?

       G   F
Are you OK, Annie?   Annie, are you OK?

                  G
So, Annie, are you OK? Are you OK, Annie?

F
   Annie, are you OK? So, Annie, are you OK?

       G   F
Are you OK, Annie?   Annie, are you OK?

          E7sus4   E   Am
So, Annie, are you OK? Are you OK, An - nie?"

Verse 2

Am   G   F   G
"Annie, are you OK? Will you tell us that you're OK?

Am   G   F
  There's a sign in the window that he struck you,

      E   Am
A cre - scendo, An - nie.

            G
He came into your a - partment.

      F   G
He left the bloodstains on the carpet.

Am   G
  Then you ran into the bedroom,

      F   E
You were struck down. It was your dorm."

Chorus 2

       F
    "Annie, are you OK? So, Annie, are you OK?

      G   **F**
Are you OK, Annie?   Annie, are you OK?

                  G
So, Annie, are you OK? Are you OK, Annie?

F
    Annie, are you OK? So, Annie, are you OK?

      G   **F**
Are you OK, Annie?

E   **Am**
You've been hit by, you've been hit by a smooth crimi - nal."

| Am G/B | C G Am | G/B | C G Am |

Verse 3

Am   **G/B**
    So, they came into the outway,

        C   **G**
It was Sunday, what a black day.

Am   **G/B**
    Mouth to mouth resusci - tation,

        C   **G**
Sounding heartbeats, intimi - dations.

Chorus 3   *Repeat Chorus 1*

Verse 4   *Repeat Verse 2*

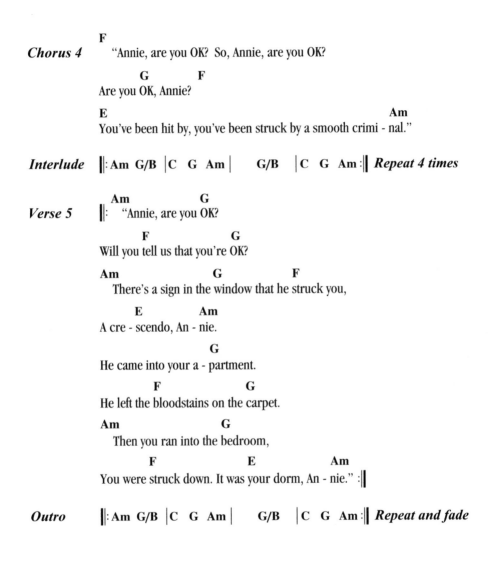

F

Chorus 4   "Annie, are you OK? So, Annie, are you OK?

       G   **F**

Are you OK, Annie?

E   **Am**

You've been hit by, you've been struck by a smooth crimi - nal."

Interlude   ‖: Am G/B │C G Am │   G/B │C G Am :‖ *Repeat 4 times*

      Am   **G**

Verse 5   ‖: "Annie, are you OK?

       F   **G**

Will you tell us that you're OK?

Am   **G**   **F**

There's a sign in the window that he struck you,

      E   **Am**

A cre - scendo, An - nie.

          G

He came into your a - partment.

      F   **G**

He left the bloodstains on the carpet.

Am   **G**

Then you ran into the bedroom,

      F   **E**   **Am**

You were struck down. It was your dorm, An - nie." :‖

Outro   ‖: Am G/B │C G Am │   G/B │C G Am :‖ *Repeat and fade*

Thriller

Words and Music by
Rod Temperton

Melody:

It's close to mid - night ___

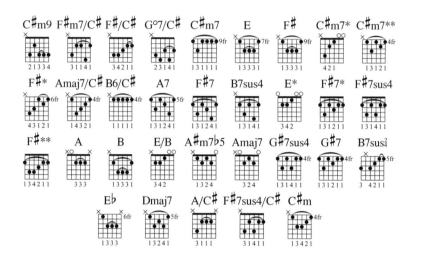

C#m9 F#m7/C# F#/C# G°7/C# C#m7 E F# C#m7* C#m7**

F#* Amaj7/C# B6/C# A7 F#7 B7sus4 E* F#7* F#7sus4

F#** A B E/B A#m7♭5 Amaj7 G#7sus4 G#7 B7sus⅔

E♭ Dmaj7 A/C# F#7sus4/C# C#m

Intro

| C#m9 | | F#m7/C# | | |

| F#/C# | | G°7/C# | | |

| C#m7 E | F# C#m7 ‖: | | :‖ *Play 4 times*

Verse 1

   F#/C#   **C#m7***
It's close to midnight and something evil's lurking in the dark.

   F#/C#   **C#m7***
Under the moonlight, you see a sight that almost stops your heart.

         F#/C#   **C#m7****
You try to scream ___ but terror takes the sound before you make ___ it.

         F#*   **Amaj7/C#**
You start to freeze ___ as horror looks you right between the eyes,

         B6/C#
You're paralyzed.

Chorus 1

C#m7 E   F# C#m7
'Cause this is thrill - er, thrill - er night.

F#/C#   F#m7/C#
And no one's gonna save you from the beast ____ about to strike.

C#m7 E   F# C#m7
You know it's thrill - er, thrill - er night.

F#/C#   A7   F#7   B7sus4   C#m7**
You're fighting for your life inside a   killer,   thriller   tonight.

Verse 2

F#/C#
Ooh, you hear the door slam

C#m7*
And realize there's nowhere left to run.

F#/C#   C#m7*
You feel the cold hand and wonder if you'll ever see the sun.

F#/C#   C#m7**
You close your eyes ____ and hope that this is just imagi - nation.

F#*   Amaj7/C#
But all the while, ____ you hear a creature creeping up behind,

B6/C#
You're out of time.

Chorus 2

C#m7 E   F# C#m7
'Cause this is thrill - er, thrill - er night.

F#/C#   F#m7/C#
There ain't no second chances 'gainst the thing with forty eyes, girl.

C#m7 E   F# C#m7
Thrill - er, thrill - er night.

F#/C#   A7   F#7   B7sus4   C#m7**
You're fighting for your life inside a   killer,   thriller   tonight.

Bridge

E* F#7*
Night creatures call

F#7sus4   F#** E* A
And the dead start to walk in their masquerade.

B C#m7**   E/B   A#m7b5
There's no escaping the jaws on the alien this time.

Amaj7   G#7sus4   G#7
This is the end of your life.

Verse 3

F#/C#
    They're out to get you.

  C#m7*
There's demons closing in on ev'ry side.

F#/C#
    They will possess you

  C#m7*
Un - less you change that number on your dial.

      F#/C#   C#m7**
Now is the time __ for you and I to cuddle close togeth - er, yeah.

        F#*   Amaj7/C#
All through the night __ I'll save you from the terror on the screen.

      B6/C#
I'll make you see...

Chorus 3

     C#m7 E   F# C#m7
That this is thrill - er, thrill - er night.

    F#/C#   F#m7/C#
'Cause I can thrill you more than any ghost ___ would ever dare try.

C#m7 E   F# C#m7
Thrill - er, thrill - er night.

  F#/C#   A7   F#7   B7sus²
So let me hold you tight and share a   killer,   thriller,

      Eb   Dmaj7   B7sus4
Chiller thriller   here tonight.

      C#m7 E   F# C#m7
'Cause this is thrill - er, thrill - er night.

   F#/C#   F#m7/C#
'Cause I can thrill you more than any ghost ___ would ever dare try.

C#m7 E   F# C#m7
Thrill - er, thrill - er night.

  F#/C#   A7   F#7
So let me hold you tight and share a killer, thriller.

Interlude | C#m7** | | | |

I'm gonna thrill you to -

Outro

C#m7**   A/C#   F#7sus4/C#

Night. *Darkness __ falls across the land,*

       F#/C#

The midnight hour is close at hand.

C#m7**   A/C#

 Creatures crawl in search of blood

F#7sus4/C#   F#/C#

 To terrorize y'all's neighborhood.

C#m7**   A/C#

 And whosoever shall be found

     F#7sus4/C#   F#/C#

Without the soul for getting down

     C#m7**   A/C#

Must stand and face the hounds of hell __ and rot

F#7sus4/C#   F#/C#

 Inside a corpse's shell.

           C#m7** A/C#

‖: I'm gonna thrill you to - night. Oo, __ baby,

      F#7sus4/C#   F#/C#

I'm gonna thrill you tonight. Oh, dar - lin', :‖

     C#m7   A/C#

Thriller night, __ baby. Oo.

     F#7sus4/C#

The foulest __ stench is in the air,

  F#/C#   C#m7**

The funk of forty thousand years,

     A/C#   F#7sus4/C# F#/C#

And grizzly ghouls from every tomb are closing in to seal your doom.

C#m7**   A/C#   F#7sus4/C#   F#/C#

 And though you fight   to stay alive, your body starts to shiver.

   C#m7**   A/C#   F#7sus4/C# F#/C#   C#m N.C.

For no mere mortal can resist the evil of the ___ thriller.

Wanna Be Startin' Somethin'

Words and Music by
Michael Jackson

I said you wan-na be start-in' some-thin',

D/E   E

Intro

| N.C. | | | | |
| D/E | E | D/E | E | |

N.C.

Chorus 1   I said you wanna be startin' somethin',

You got to be startin' somethin'.

I said you wanna be startin' somethin',

You got to be startin' somethin'.

        D/E
It's too high ____ to get over, (Yeah, yeah.)

     E
It's too low ____ to get under. (Yeah, yeah.)

        D/E
You're stuck ____ in the middle (Yeah, yeah.)

      E
And the pain ____ is thunder. (Yeah, yeah.)

Verse 1

N.C.
I took my ___ baby to the doctor with a fever,

But, nothing he found.

By the time this hit the street,

They said she had a breakdown.

D/E   E
Some - one's always tryin' to start ___ my baby cryin'.

D/E   E
Talk - in', squealin', lyin', *sayin' you*

Just wanna be startin' somethin'.

Chorus 2

N.C.
I said you wanna be startin' somethin',

You got to be startin' somethin'.

I said you wanna be startin' somethin',

You got to be startin' somethin'.

D/E
‖: It's too high ___ to get over, (Yeah, yeah.)

E
It's too low ___ to get under. (Yeah, yeah.)

D/E
You're stuck ___ in the middle (Yeah, yeah.)

E
And the pain ___ is thunder. (Yeah, yeah.) :‖

Verse 2

N.C.
Billie Jean ___ is always talkin'

When nobody else is talkin'.

Tellin' lies and rubbin' shoulders,

So they called her mouth a motor.

D/E   E
Some - one's always tryin' to start ___ my baby cryin',

D/E   E
Talk - in', squealin', spyin', sayin' you

Just wanna be startin' somethin'.

Chorus 3

N.C.
I said you wanna be startin' somethin',

You got to be startin' somethin'.

I said you wanna be startin' somethin',

You got to be startin' somethin'.

                D/E
‖: It's too high ____ to get over, (Yeah, yeah.)

          E
It's too low ____ to get under. (Yeah, yeah.)

            D/E
You're stuck ____ in the middle (Yeah, yeah.)

          E
And the pain ____ is thunder. (Yeah, yeah.) :‖

        D/E
You're a veg'table. (You're a veg'table.)

        E
You're a veg'table. (You're a veg'table.)

        D/E
Still they hate you. (Still they hate you.)

        E
You're a veg'table. (You're a veg'table.)

        D/E
You're the buffet. (You're the buffet.)

        E
You're a veg'table. (You're a veg'table.)

        D/E
They eat off ____ of you. (They eat off of you.)

      E
You're a veg'table.

Interlude

‖: N.C. | | | :‖
| D/E | E | D/E | E |

Verse 3

N.C.

If you can't ___ feed your baby (Yeah, yeah.)

Then don't have a baby. (Yeah, yeah.)

And don't think maybe (Yeah, yeah.)

If you can't feed your baby. (Yeah, yeah.)

D/E   E
You'll ___be always tryin' to stop ___ that child from cryin'.

D/E   E
Hust - lin', stealin', lyin', now baby's slowly dyin'.

Chorus 4

N.C.

I said you wanna be startin' somethin',

You got to be startin' somethin'.

I said you wanna be startin' somethin',

You got to be startin' somethin'.

D/E
‖: It's too high ___ to get over, (Yeah, yeah.)

E
It's too low ___ to get under. (Yeah, yeah.)

D/E
You're stuck ___ in the middle (Yeah, yeah.)

E
And the pain ___ is thunder. (Yeah, yeah.) :‖

D/E   E
Lift your head ___ up high and scream out to ___ the world,

D/E   E
"I know I am ___ someone!" and let the truth ___ unfurl.

D/E   E
No one can hurt ___ you now because you know ___ it's true.

D/E   E
Yes, I believe ___ in me, so you believe ___ in you.

Help me sing it.

Outro

D/E
‖: (Ma ma se, ma ma sa, ma ma ma coo sa.

E
Ma ma se, ma ma sa, ma ma ma coo sa.) :‖ *Repeat and fade*
w/ lead vocal ad lib.

The Way You Make Me Feel

Words and Music by
Michael Jackson

(Capo 1st fret)

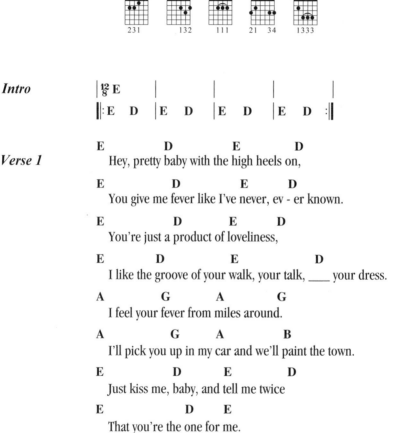

Intro

| 12/8 E | | | | |

‖: E D | E D | E D | E D :‖

Verse 1

E   D   E   D
Hey, pretty baby with the high heels on,

E   D   E   D
You give me fever like I've never, ev - er known.

E   D   E   D
You're just a product of loveliness,

E   D   E   D
I like the groove of your walk, your talk, ___ your dress.

A   G   A   G
I feel your fever from miles around.

A   G   A   B
I'll pick you up in my car and we'll paint the town.

E   D   E   D
Just kiss me, baby, and tell me twice

E   D   E
That you're the one for me.

Chorus 1

N.C.   E   D   E
The way you make me feel. ___ (The way you make me feel.)

       D   E   D   E
You really turn me on. ___ (You really turn me on.)

        D   E   D   E
You knock me off of my feet. ___ (You knock me off of my feet.)

       D   E   D   E D
My lonely days are gone. ___ (My lonely days are gone.)

Verse 2

E   D   E   D
I like the feelin' you're givin' me,

E   D   E   D
Just hold me, baby, and I'm in ec - stasy.

E   D   E   D
Oh, I'll be workin' from nine to five

E   D   E   D
To buy you things to keep you by ___ my side.

A   G   A   G
I never felt so in love before.

A   G   A   B
Just promise, baby, you'll love me for - evermore.

E   D   E   D
I swear I'm keeping you satisfied,

E   D   E
'Cause you're the one for me.

Chorus 2

N.C.   E   D   E
The way you make me feel. ___ (The way you make me feel.)

       D   E   D   E
You really turn me on. ___ (You really turn me on.)

        D   E   D   E
You knock me off of my feet. ___ (You knock me off of my feet.)

       D   E   D   E N.C.
My lonely days are gone. ___ (My lonely days are gone.)

Instrumental   ‖: E   D | E   D | E   D | E   D   :‖

         A   G   A   G

Verse 3   I never felt so in love before.

         A   G   A   B

Just promise, baby, you'll love me for - evermore.

        E   D   E   D

I swear I'm keeping you satisfied,

        E   D   E

'Cause you're the one for me.

        N.C.   E   D   E

Chorus 3   The way you make me feel. ___ (The way you make me feel.)

               D   E   D   E

You really turn me on. ___ (You really turn me on.)

               D   E   D   E

You knock me off of my feet. ___ (You knock me off of my feet.)

               D   E   D   E

My lonely days are gone. ___ (My lonely days are gone.)

             D

Ain't ___ nobody's bus'ness.

        E   D   E D

Outro-Chorus   ‖: (The way you make me feel.

        E   D   E D

You really turn me on.

        E   D   E D

You knock me off of my feet.

        E   D   E D

My lonely days are gone.)   :‖ *Repeat and fade*
                                          w/ lead vocal ad lib.

Will You Be There

Words and Music by
Michael Jackson

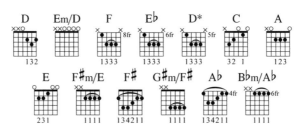

Intro

|D Em/D |D Em/D |D Em/D |D Em/D |

D Em/D   D Em/D
Ooh, ooh, ooh, ooh, ooh, ooh, ooh, ooh,

D Em/D   D Em/D
Ooh, ooh, ooh, ooh, ooh, ooh.

Verse 1

D   Em/D D
Hold me like the River   Jordan,

    Em/D   D
And I will then say to thee

Em/D   D Em/D
You are my friend.

D   Em/D   D
Carry me like you are my brother.

    Em/D   D
Love me like a mother.

Em/D   D Em/D
Will you be there?

Interlude 1

      D Em/D   D Em/D
‖: Ooh, ooh, ooh, ooh, ooh, ooh, ooh, ooh,

D Em/D   D Em/D
Ooh, ooh, ooh, ooh, ooh, ooh.   :‖

Verse 2

          D   Em/D   D
When weary, tell me will you hold me?

          Em/D   D
When wrong, will you scold me?

          Em/D   D   Em/D
When lost will you find me?

          D   Em/D   D
But they told me a man should be faithful

          Em/D   D
And walk when not able

          Em/D   D
And fight 'til the end

               Em/D
But I'm only human.

Interlude 2   *Repeat Interlude 1*

Bridge

F   E♭   D*
Ev'ryone's taking con - trol of me,

F   E♭   D*
Seems that the world's got a role for me.

F   E♭   D*
I'm so con - fused, will you show to me

               C   A
You'll be there for me and care enough to bear me.

Verse 3

     E   F♯m/E   E
(Hold me, lay your head lowly.

F♯m/E   E   F♯m/E   E   F♯m/E
Softly and boldly carry me there.

E   F♯m/E   E
Hold me, love me and feed me.

F♯m/E   E   F♯m/E   E   F♯m/E
Kiss me and free me. I will feel blessed.)

Verse 4

F♯   G♯m/F♯ F♯
(Carry, carry me boldly.

G♯m/F♯ F♯
Lift me up slowly.

G♯m/F♯ F♯   G♯m/F♯
Carry me there.

F♯   G♯m/F♯   F♯
Save me, heal me and bathe me,

G♯m/F♯ F♯
Softly you say to me

G♯m/F♯ F♯   G♯m/F♯
I will be   there.)

Verse 5

A♭   B♭m/A♭ A♭
(Lift me, lift me up slowly.

B♭m/A♭ A♭
Carry me boldly.

B♭m/A♭   A♭ B♭m/A♭
Show me you care.)

A♭   B♭m/A♭   A♭
Hold me, lay your head lowly.

B♭m/A♭ A♭
Softly then boldly,

B♭m/A♭ A♭ B♭m/A♭
Carry me there.

A♭   B♭m/A♭   A♭
Need me, love me and feed me.

B♭m/A♭   A♭
Kiss me and free me.

B♭m/A♭ A♭   B♭m/A♭ A♭
I will feel blessed.)

You Rock My World

Words and Music by Michael Jackson,
Fred Jerkins III, Lashawn Ameen Daniels,
Rodney Jerkins and Nora Payne

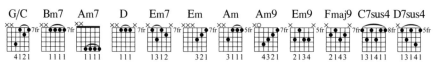

My life will nev-er be __ the same

G/C   Bm7   Am7   D   Em7   Em   Am   Am9   Em9   Fmaj9   C7sus4   D7sus4

Intro

| N.C.(Em7) | $\frac{2}{4}$ | $\frac{4}{4}$ (Am7) | (Em7) | |
| (Am7) | (Em7) | G/C Bm7 | |
‖: Am7   D | Em7   G/C Bm7 :‖ *Play 5 times*
| Am7   D | Em7 | |

Verse 1

          Am
My life will never be the same

D   **Em**
  'Cause girl, you came and changed

    Am   **D**
The way I walk, the way I talk.

Em   **Am**
I cannot explain these things I feel for you.

D   **Em**
  But girl, you know it's true.

Am
Stay with me, fulfill my dreams

D   **Em**
  And I'll be all you need.

G/C Bm7 Am7
      Feels so right.

D Em7   **G/C Bm7 Am7**
  I've searched for the per - fect   love all my life.

D Em7   **G/C Bm7 Am7**
  Oh, ooh,   feels like I

D Em7   **G/C Bm7 Am7**
  Have finally found a _____ perfect love this time.

          D   **Em7**
I've finally found, ___ so come on, girl.

Chorus 1

     G/C   **Bm7 Am7**
You rocked my   world, you know you did,

        D Em7
And ev - 'ry - thing I own I give.

     G/C Bm7 Am7
The rar - est   love, who'd think I'd find

         D   **Em7**
Someone like ____ you ____ to call mine?

     G/C   **Bm7 Am7**
You rocked my   world, you know you did,

        D Em7
And ev - 'ry - thing I own I give.

     G/C Bm7 Am7
The rar - est   love, who'd think I'd find

         D   **Em7**
Someone like ____ you ____ to call mine?

Verse 2

      N.C.   **Am**
In time I knew that love would bring

D   **Em**
  Such happiness to me.

 Am   **D**   **Em**
I tried to keep my sanity.   I've waited patiently.

Am   **D**   **Em**
Girl, you know it seems   my life is so complete.

  Am
A love that's true because of you.

D   **Em**
  Keep doin' what you do.

G/C Bm7 Am7
        Think that I've

D Em7   **G/C**
  Fin'lly found the perfect love

Bm7 Am7
I've   searched for all my life.

D Em7   **G/C Bm7 Am7**
  Oh, who'd   think I'd find

D Em7   **G/C Bm7 Am7**
  Such a perfect love that's ____awesomely so right.

  D Em7
Oh, girl.

Chorus 2

      G/C   **Bm7** **Am7**
‖: You rocked my   world, you know you did,

            D **Em7**
And ev - 'ry - thing I own I give.

      G/C **Bm7 Am7**
The rar - est   love, who'd think I'd find

               D   **Em7**
Someone like ___ you ___ to call mine? :‖ ***Play 4 times***

Bridge

G/C Am9 Bm7   **Em9**
Girl,   I know ___ that this is love.

Bm7 **G/C**   **Am9** **D**   **Em9**
 I felt ___ the magic's all ___ in ___ the air.

Fmaj9   **G/C Am9 Bm7**   **Em9**
 And girl, ___   I'll nev - er get enough,

Bm7   **C7sus4**   **D7sus4**
 That's why ___ I always have to have you here.

Chorus 3   *Repeat Chorus 2*

Interlude   ‖: **N.C.** | :‖

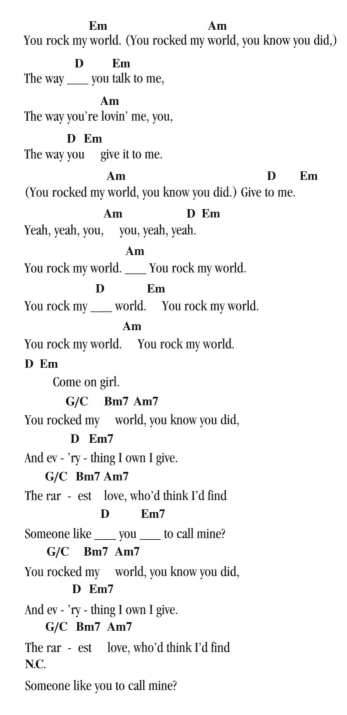

Chorus 4

                Em   **Am**
You rock my world. (You rocked my world, you know you did,)

        D   **Em**
The way ____ you talk to me,

           Am
The way you're lovin' me, you,

        D **Em**
The way you   give it to me.

             Am   **D**   **Em**
(You rocked my world, you know you did.) Give to me.

             Am   **D Em**
Yeah, yeah, you,   you, yeah, yeah.

                Am
You rock my world. ____ You rock my world.

           D   **Em**
You rock my ____ world.   You rock my world.

                Am
You rock my world.   You rock my world.

D Em
    Come on girl.

        G/C   **Bm7 Am7**
You rocked my   world, you know you did,

        D Em7
And ev - 'ry - thing I own I give.

      G/C Bm7 Am7
The rar - est   love, who'd think I'd find

           D   **Em7**
Someone like ____ you ____ to call mine?

    G/C   **Bm7 Am7**
You rocked my   world, you know you did,

        D Em7
And ev - 'ry - thing I own I give.

    G/C Bm7 Am7
The rar - est   love, who'd think I'd find
N.C.

Someone like you to call mine?

You Are Not Alone

Words and Music by
Robert Kelly

Melody:

An - oth - er day _ has gone, _

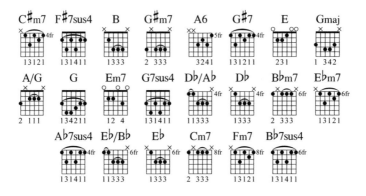

C#m7 F#7sus4 B G#m7 A6 G#7 E Gmaj

A/G G Em7 G7sus4 Db/Ab Db Bbm7 Ebm7

Ab7sus4 Eb/Bb Eb Cm7 Fm7 Bb7sus4

Intro
| C#m7 | F#7sus4 |

Verse 1

   F#7sus4   B   G#m7
Another day has gone, ____ I'm still all alone.

            C#m7   F#7sus4
How could this be, ___ you're not here with me?

                B   G#m7
You never said goodbye. ____ Someone tell me why

          C#m7   F#7sus4
Did she have to go ____ and leave my world so cold?

   A6   G#7
Ev'ry day I sit and ask myself

   E
How did love slip away?

C#m7   F#7sus4
Something whispers in my ear and says…

Chorus 1

                                        B   **G♯m7**
That you are not alone, ____ I am here with you.

                               C♯m7   **F♯7sus4**
Though you're far away ____ I am here to stay.

                          B   **G♯m7**
You are not alone, ____ I am here with you.

                             C♯m7   **F♯7sus4**
Though we're far apart ____ you're always in my heart.

                            B   **Gmaj7** **A/G**   **B**
But you are not alone, ____ lone, _____ lone.

       Gmaj7 **F♯7sus4**
Why alone?

Verse 2

                          B   **G♯m7**
Just the other night ____ I thought I heard you cry

                      C♯m7   **F♯7sus4**
Asking me to come ____ and hold you in my arms.

                            B   **G♯m7**
I can hear your breaths, ____ your burdens I will bear,

                      C♯m7   **F♯7sus4**
But first I need you here ____ then forever can begin.

       A6   **G♯7**
Ev'ry day I sit and ask myself

       E
How did love slip away?

C♯m7   **F♯7sus4**
Something whispers in my ear and says…

Chorus 2

                            B   **G♯m7**
That you are not alone, ___ I am here with you.

                           C♯m7   **F♯7sus4**
Though you're far away ___ I am here to stay.

                      B   **G♯m7**
You are not alone, ___ I am here with you.

                      C♯m7   **F♯7sus4**
Though we're far apart ___ you're always in my heart.

                      B
But you are not alone.

Bridge

       G   **A/G**   **Em7**
Oh,   whisper three words ___ then I'll come runnin',

 Gmaj7   **A/G**   **F♯7sus4**
I,   and girl you know ___ that I'll be there

   G7sus4
I'll be there.

Chorus 3

N.C.(D♭/A♭)   **D♭**   **B♭m7**
You are not alone, ___ I am here with you.

                    E♭m7   **A♭7sus4**
Though you're far away ___ I am here to stay.

                D♭   **B♭m7**
You are not alone, ___ I am here with you.

                  E♭m7   **A♭7sus4**
Though we're far apart ___ you're always in my heart.

Chorus 4

  E♭/B♭   **E♭**   **Cm7**
But you are not alone, ___ I am here with you.

                  Fm7   **B♭7sus4**
Though you're far away ___ I am here to stay.

                 E♭   **Cm7**
You are not alone, ___ I am here with you.

                Fm7   **B♭7sus4**
Though we're far apart ___ you're always in my heart.

                E♭
You are not alone.   *Fade out*

This series will help you play your favorite songs quickly and easily. Just follow the tab and listen to the audio to the hear how the guitar should sound, and then play along using the separate backing tracks. Mac or PC users can also slow down the tempo without changing pitch by using the CD in their computer. The melody and lyrics are included in the book so that you can sing or simply follow along.

INCLUDES TAB

Complete series list and song lists available online

Prices, contents, and availability subject to change without notice.

HAL•LEONARD®
CORPORATION

7777 W. BLUEMOUND RD. P.O. BOX 13819 MILWAUKEE, WI 53213

www.halleonard.com